Tort Law in the United States

Tort Law in the United States

Fifth Edition

H. Beau Baez III

This book was originally published as a monograph in the International Encyclopaedia of Laws/Tort Law.

Founding Editor: Roger Blanpain†
General Editor: Frank Hendrickx
Volume Editor: Britt Weyts

Wolters Kluwer

Published by:
Kluwer Law International B.V.
PO Box 316
2400 AH Alphen aan den Rijn
The Netherlands
E-mail: lrs-sales@wolterskluwer.com
Website: www.wolterskluwer.com/en/solutions/kluwerlawinternational

Sold and distributed by:
Wolters Kluwer Legal & Regulatory U.S.
920 Links Avenue
Landisville, PA 17538
United States of America
E-mail: customer.service@wolterskluwer.com

ISBN 978-94-035-6240-7

e-Book: ISBN 978-94-035-6250-6
web-PDF: ISBN 978-94-035-6260-5

This title is available on www.kluwerlawonline.com

The Author

H. Beau Baez III was born in Miami, Florida, USA. He received his BA and BS from Liberty University, Virginia, and JD & LLM from Georgetown University, Washington, D.C. He began his academic career at Concord School of Law and has since been on the faculties at Liberty University, Charlotte School of Law, University of North Dakota, University of Northern Illinois, University of Idaho, and he is currently at Ohio Northern University.

Professor Baez is a member of the following bars: the Supreme Court of the United States, the United States Court of Federal Claims, the United States Tax Court, and the District of Columbia Court of Appeals. In 2009, he was appointed to the North Carolina General Statutes Commission, where he served until 2017. He is also the author of numerous scholarly articles and books. He also blogs at Law School Tips, https://learnlawbetter.com/law-school-tips and has a YouTube channel with viewers in over 150 countries: https://www.youtube.com/learnlawbetter.

The Author

Table of Contents

Table of Contents

List of Abbreviations

GDP	Gross Domestic Product
PREP Act	Public Readiness and Emergency Preparedness Act

List of Abbreviations

General Introduction

§1. The General Background of the Country

I. Geography[1]

1. Based on the total area, the United States is the third-largest country in the world, behind Canada and Russia. The United States is located in the western hemisphere and is composed of forty-eight contiguous states, Alaska, and Hawaii, and holds recognized territories in Guam, Puerto Rico, and the United States Virgin Islands, as well as several other unorganized overseas territories, including those in Micronesia and American Samoa. The total area of the United States is 9,826,630 square kilometers of land and water area, and shares land borders in the north with Canada, south with Mexico, water borders with Russia in the northwest and the Bahamas in the southeast. The capital of the United States is Washington, District of Columbia, with a population of 702,250 as of July 1, 2024.

As of November 10, 2025, the United States had a total population of 342,801,792.

II. History[2]

2. The origin of the United States is recent and somewhat disputed. Historians and other scholars disagree about the migration patterns of persons to North and South America, whether by land across the Bering Strait or by sea via the Atlantic Ocean. Most, however, concede that at least by the tenth century, there were persons living in the Americas of Asian and European descent, who would be referred to as "Indians" when explorations of the 1400s and 1500s resulted in misreported discoveries of the East Indies. In September 1565, Europeans established the first permanent settlement in what is now the United States, when the Spanish explorer, Pedro Menendez de Aviles, discovered and established St. Augustine, Florida. Subsequently, in 1607, the English established their first permanent American colony in Jamestown, Virginia. In such a manner, the European countries of Spain, France, and England (with minor and historically inconsequential colonization attempts by

1. United States Central Intelligence Agency, *World Factbook: United States*, www.cia.gov/ library/ publications/the-world-factbook/geos/US.html (Oct. 25, 2019); United States Census Bureau, *United States Census Bureau: Population Estimates*, http://www.census.gov/popest/data/national/ totals/2012/index.html (Aug. 24, 2013).
2. R. Remini, *A Short History of the United States* 1 (HarperCollins 2008).

other European countries) established numerous colonies with separate allegiances and legal systems throughout what is now collectively the United States.

In 1686, King James II created the Dominion of New England, composed of the colonies of Massachusetts, Rhode Island, Connecticut, New Hampshire, and later New York and New Jersey. Unlike prior English colonies that were controlled by one governor each, all of the colonies in the Dominion were controlled together by a solitary and dictatorial governor, Sir Edmund Andros, to whom King James II gave the power to legislate and levy taxes for England. When King James II was overthrown in the Glorious Revolution of 1688, the colonists dismantled the Dominion of New England, arrested Andros, and reestablished their individual governments. England, however, still attempted to exercise tight political control over the colonies and to expand its territory in North America, as did France and Spain. These conflicting expansions resulted in several wars, including the Seven Years War (called the French and Indian War in the American colonies) between the English and French, which ended in 1763 and left England in control of the colonies that would later become the first thirteen states of the United States. By this time, however, the Great Awakening had spurred concepts of individualism in the colonists, not just religiously, but politically as well, which only intensified the political power struggle between England and the colonies.

3. In 1763, largely to pacify increasing tension with the Indians, the English issued the Proclamation of 1763, which prohibited further colonial expansion west of the Appalachian Mountains. England then passed a series of acts—the Sugar Act, Quartering Act, Stamp Act, and Declaratory Act—in a further attempt to exercise political control over the colonists, who increasingly desired political independence. The colonists unified in protest of the Stamp Act, which required them to pay taxes to England and which they regarded as "taxation without representation," a clear oracle of tyranny. Their formal protests through the Stamp Act Congress led to England's repeal of the Stamp Act and demonstrated the power the colonists had when they worked together as a unified assembly. England, however, did not stop trying to control and tax the colonists, and the colonists' response to a tea tax resulted in even stricter English control when the English Parliament enacted the Coercive Laws or Intolerable Acts in the spring of 1774.

In response to the Coercive Laws, representatives from all of the thirteen then-existing colonies except Georgia assembled in the First Continental Congress in Philadelphia, Pennsylvania, on September 5, 1774. Out of this assembly, the colonists reaffirmed their position that the colonies were not strictly English territories but were independent sovereign states. The Second Continental Congress convened on May 10, 1775, at which the representatives formed an army, appointed George Washington as General, issued currency, and began their own foreign negotiations. Thereafter, the colonists began to actively seek complete independence from England, leading to the American Revolutionary War. On July 4, 1776, the Continental Congress adopted the Declaration of Independence setting forth the United States' sovereignty from England. After a long war, the English recognized the sovereignty of its former colonies on November 30, 1782, by means of a treaty between England and the United States.

4. The first governing document for the United States, the Articles of Confederation, proved too weak to handle the rising issues facing the states, and the Continental Congress invited the thirteen states to send representatives to a special convention in Philadelphia, Pennsylvania in 1787 for the purpose of constituting a workable federal government.

In May 1787, the United States Constitutional Convention met. Over the next several months, the members of the Convention debated, drafted, and finalized a federal Constitution. By July 26, 1788, eleven of the thirteen states had ratified the Constitution, which replaced the Articles of Confederation in those states. The remaining two states ratified the Constitution shortly thereafter. This Constitution set up a central tripartite federal government, and on the first Wednesday of February 1789, George Washington and John Adams were elected as the first President and Vice President of the United States of America. The first Congress under the new federal Constitution raised revenue; established the State, Treasury, and Defense Departments; created the federal judiciary system; created the Attorney General's office; and passed a Bill of Rights, ten of the original twelve suggested amendments, which were ratified by the states on December 15, 1791.

5. During the early part of the nineteenth century, the United States continued its expansion by acquiring the Louisiana Territory and West Florida from the French in 1803. However, while growing and asserting itself as a nation, the United States was increasingly faced with global pressures from England and France, who were then at war with one another, and who each sought the United States' allegiance and assistance. The United States, of which there were then nineteen Member States, initially resolved to remain neutral through congressionally imposed trade restrictions on both countries. This attempt at neutrality, however, failed, and after Napoleon's abdication, England redirected its military efforts from France to the United States, leading to the War of 1812.

After the War of 1812, the United States gained global recognition as a new world power, and a sense of national patriotism developed. The years following sparked literary, industrial, and transportation revolutions in the United States. During this time, the United States also experienced significant political change, moving from a one-party republican government toward a bipartisan democratic government.

6. After Congress passed the Tariff of 1828, the United States entered a period of turmoil regarding the appropriate balance of powers between federal and state governments. On December 29, 1845, Texas became a state, and, following the Mexican-American War, the United States also acquired the present states of Arizona, California, Nevada, Utah, and New Mexico, as well as parts of Colorado and Wyoming. Following this significant territorial expansion, Congress battled for several years over the issue of whether to allow slavery in the newly acquired states, with tensions ever increasing over the issue.

When Abraham Lincoln was elected President of the United States in 1860, the southern states immediately began seceding from the United States. The seceded states established the Confederate States of America in 1861, recognizing each Member State as an independent sovereign. This led to the War Between the States or Civil War, which claimed the lives of more than 600,000 Americans and which continued until the Confederacy surrendered on April 9, 1865. After the war, the United States amended its Constitution to outlaw slavery and to prevent further ongoing racial discrimination.[3] Following the end of the Civil War, the United States continued its expansion, acquiring Alaska in 1867; Puerto Rico, Guam, the Philippines, and Hawaii in 1898; and the Virgin Islands in 1917.

7. In the late nineteenth century and into the early twentieth century, while continuing to expand its presence and power globally, the United States attempted unsuccessfully to assert itself as a neutral nation with regard to international disputes, even during the early years of World War I. However, after Germany sank three American merchantmen, the United States entered World War I on April 6, 1917. At the conclusion of the war, Americans returned to their prior isolationist views and continued to avoid involvement in global affairs.

During the Great Depression, which began with the stock market crash of 1929, the governmental branches became increasingly conflicted over their balance of powers, particularly with the expanding authority of the Executive Branch under Franklin D. Roosevelt's presidency. During Roosevelt's presidency, the United States moved away from a purer form of capitalism and adopted many of the ideas of the Progressive Era, such as child labor laws and workers' compensation laws.

Although Americans still desired to avoid involvement in foreign affairs, fascism and communism were evolving as international concerns. Roosevelt, while against direct involvement in the overseas conflict, regarded the United States as "the great arsenal of democracy" and made it clear that the United States would protect democracy, even if that entailed entering another war. After suffering a military defeat when Japan attacked Pearl Harbor, Hawaii, and other United States territories in the Pacific Ocean on December 7, 1941, the United States begrudgingly entered World War II by declaring war on Japan—within a few days Germany and Italy declared war on the United States. In 1945, World War II ended in defeat for Germany and Japan, and the United States ratified the United Nations Charter, committing itself for the first time to a policy of international cooperation, a significant departure from its previous isolationistic perspective.

8. Since fascism was no longer considered an immediate threat, the United States directed its military efforts at preventing the spread of communism, which Americans regarded as the most significant ongoing threat to the preservation of democracy. On July 21, 1949, the United States signed its first cooperative international treaty, the North Atlantic Treaty, which established the North Atlantic Treaty Organization, and which provided that a war declared on any member nation was a war declared on all. This alliance marked the beginning of the United States' international position as the preserver of democracy, a position demonstrated by its involvement in the Korean Conflict and the Vietnam War.

---

3. *See* U.S. Const. Amends. XIII–XIV. These amendments are traditionally referred to as the Civil War Amendments, ratified respectively in 1865, 1868, and 1870. The former confederate states were allowed to rejoin the United States after the war between the States, dependent on their ratification of these amendments.

III. Political System

9. The United States Constitution is the highest level of positive law in the United States, and all federal law, treaties with foreign governments, and subnational law (i.e., state and local law) must conform to the Constitution.[4] Amending the Constitution is difficult and has occurred only twenty-seven times, ten of those times in the eighteenth century.

10. Guiding principles of the United States Constitution are:

- the republican principle;
- the democratic principle;
- federalism;
- separated powers;
- checks and balances; and
- the fundamental notion of human equality.

Together, these principles form the basis of the United States constitutional order. In 1787, John Adams defined republicanism as:

> a government in which the property of the people predominated and governed .... This idea, indeed, implies liberty; because property cannot be secure, unless the man be at liberty to acquire, use, or part with it, at his discretion, and unless he [has] his personal liberty of life and limb, motion and rest, for that purpose; it implies, moreover, that the property and liberty of all men, not merely of a majority, should be safe; for the people or public, comprehends more than a majority, it comprehends all and every individual: and the property of every citizen is a part of the public property, as each citizen is a part of the public, people, or community.[5]

This concept of republicanism remains a principle of the United States constitutional order, having established a federal government limited to certain enumerated (yet broad) powers, those powers not so enumerated remaining with the states or the people collectively.[6] Ultimately, under this principle, "the people are the fountain of all power, to whom alone it of right belongs to make or unmake constitutions, or forms of government, at their pleasure."[7] Under the principles of republicanism as established in the United States, the people exercise this power of self-governance through chosen government representatives.[8]

---

4. U.S. Const. Art. VI, cl. 2.
5. J. Adams, *A Defense of the Constitutions of Government of the United States of America*, in *Contexts of the Constitution* 250 (N. Cogan ed., Foundation Press 1996).
6. *See* U.S. Const. Amend. X.
7. Brutus, *Essay of Brutus, No. 1*, in *Contexts of the Constitution* 267 (N. Cogan ed., Foundation Press 1996).
8. *Ibid.*, 273; *See also* J. Madison, *The Federalist No. 63*, in *Contexts of the Constitution* 302 (N. Cogan ed., Foundation Press 1996).

11. The democratic principle influences United States' constitutional order as well. The United States constitutional framers defined a pure democracy as a society controlled by a small number of citizens who personally assembled and administered the government, and they preferred a republican to a democratic government because they believed a pure democracy would elevate the will of a few over the interests of the many and, as such, would be incompatible with the rights they wished to preserve for all people, such as those of personal security, property, and liberty.[9] As the United States has evolved, however, so has its idea of democracy. The modern conception of democracy includes the notion of majority rule, representation by elected officials, and the consideration of fundamental rights applicable to all citizens, including the minority.[10]

12. The principle of federalism also informs the United States' constitutional order. The Constitution assumed that the states would continue to exist as separate sovereigns even while the powers of the federal government were extensively enlarged from the Articles of Confederation.[11] Modern conceptions of federalism—the relationship between the state and federal governments—fall under two main categories: competitive theories and cooperative theories. The competitive theories of federalism include nation-centered, in which the Constitution since it was ratified by the American people as a whole, established a federal government to be the focal point of political power in the United States with a dual role of defending both the Union and the individual states; state-centered, in which the Constitution was the result of state action that created a limited federal government in order to protect the states' sovereignty; and dual federalism, in which:

> [t]he national and state governments form two separate centers of power, from each of which the other is barred and between which there is something like a jurisdictional no-man's land, into which both are barred from entering. Each government in its own sphere is sovereign, and there is an essential equality between them.[12]

Traditionally, dual federalism was the primary theory of American federalism. This dual relationship, however, still recognizes the "supremacy of the authority of the United States when any conflict arises between the two governments."[13] Cooperative conceptions of American federalism gained recognition following World

9. J. Madison, *The Federalist No. 10*, in *Contexts of the Constitution* 283 (N. Cogan ed., Foundation Press 1996).
10. R. Weise & A. de Grazia, *Eight Branches: American Government Today* 23–40 (Collegiate Publishing 1975).
11. *Ibid.*
12. R. Leach, *American Federalism* 10–14 (W.W. Norton & Co. 1970).
13. *Ibid.*

War I, in which the state and federal governments ceased being viewed as completely separate but began to consciously work together for specific ends, resulting in the concepts of concurrent powers, as in highways, and state-reserved powers, as in general police powers.[14]

13. The principles of separated powers and checks and balances are intertwined in the United States' constitutional order. The framers believed that a concentration of power in one political body was tyrannical so when they considered the three main roles of the republican government they were organizing—lawmaking, enforcing the law, and interpreting it—they created one branch for each role: the legislative, executive, and judicial branches.[15] The legislative function was placed into a bicameral legislature, the upper chamber is the Senate and the lower chamber the House of Representatives. The framers were also aware of the tendency of governmental authorities to inflate their power, so the Constitution contains checks on the power of each governmental branch.[16] For example, the executive can check the power of the legislative branch through the presidential veto power; the House of Representatives can check the presidential power by impeaching the president; and the Senate confirms all presidential nominees to the Supreme Court.[17] In addition, although not expressly stated in the Constitution, the power of judicial review set forth in *Marbury v. Madison*[18] gives the judicial branch the authority to check the legislature by striking down laws it determines are unconstitutional.[19] Aside from these checks on one another, each branch is limited to its specific powers and cannot cross over into the realm of the powers delegated to either of the other two branches. As such, the notions of separation of powers and checks and balances, when viewed in tandem, make "each organ of the government a perpetual sentinel over the other two."[20]

14. The fundamental notion of human equality also informs United States politics. As America struggled to become an independent nation, the concept of individual rights became a part of American political thought.[21] Early pre-Revolution discussions considered life, liberty, and property to be fundamental rights shared by all. From these pre-Revolution discussions sprang the Declaration of Independence in 1776 and later informed the Constitution. Although the framers disagreed about whether the Constitution should provide for these fundamental rights, they all

14. R. Weise & A. de Grazia, *Eight Branches: American Government Today* 286 (Collegiate Publishing 1975).
15. *Ibid.*, 58–59.
16. W. Ayars, *The United States Government: A Citizen's Inquiry into What It Is and Might Be* 293 (Ivy House Publishing Group 2003).
17. *Ibid.*
18. *Marbury v. Madison*, 5 U.S. 137, 176–178 (1803).
19. *Ibid.*
20. R. Weise & A. de Grazia, *Eight Branches: American Government Today* 59 (Collegiate Publishing 1975).
21. *See* R. Rutland, *The Birth of the Bill of Rights* 27 (Northeastern University Press 1983).

agreed on the existence of some basic level of human equality and that a free society could only be maintained by guaranteeing certain fundamental rights.[22] Although the concept of equality has been defined differently throughout American history, it has always been a guiding principle of the United States' constitutional order.

15. The United States Constitution describes the structure and authority of the legislative branch in Article I. The federal legislative branch is bicameral, collectively called Congress, which consists of a Senate and a House of Representatives. The House of Representatives, generally referred to as the lower house, is composed of members elected to serve a two-year term, and the number of representatives for each state is based on a state's population. The Senate, generally referred to as the upper house, is composed of two members from each state who are elected to serve a six-year term, and the Vice President of the United States also serves as the President of the Senate.[23] All impeachments by the House of Representatives are tried by the Senate.[24] The powers and responsibilities of the United States Congress include: taxation, spending, regulating commerce, and declaring war. The limitations of the United States Congress include but are not limited to: prohibitions on issuing bills of attainder, issuing ex post facto laws, suspending the writ of habeas corpus, or giving preference to one state over another.

16. The United States Constitution describes the structure and authority of the executive branch, which is primarily to ensure that the laws of the United States are faithfully executed.[25] The federal executive power is vested in a President and Vice President, who are elected to a four-year term of office.[26] The President is limited to two terms in office and is the chief representative of the United States in the global community during his time in office. The President is also Commander-in-Chief of the United States military and has the authority to pardon criminal offenses against the United States.[27] The President additionally has the authority to enter into treaties upon concurrence by two-thirds of the Senate and nominates ambassadors, public ministers, Supreme Court justices, and other executive officers of the United States.[28]

17. State governments within the United States are generally modeled after the federal government and, although the states are not constitutionally required to do so, all fifty states' governments are composed of the same three branches—executive, legislative, and judicial.[29] The executive branch in each state

22. *Ibid.*, 220–221.
23. U.S. Const. Art. I, §3, cl. 1, 4.
24. *Ibid.*, §3, cl. 6.
25. U.S. Const. Art. II, §3.
26. *Ibid.*, §1, cl. 1–5. *See* U.S. Const. Amends. XII, XX, XXII, XXIII, XXV for more discussion on the presidency and electoral process.
27. U.S. Const. Art. II, §2, cl. 1.
28. *Ibid.*, §2, cl. 2.
29. The White House, *Our Government: State and Local Government*, www.whitehouse.gov/ our_government/state_and_local_government/ (Jun. 8, 2009).

is headed by a governor, who is elected directly by that state's residents.[30] Other executive branch leaders in most states are also directly elected, although the executive structure differs from state to state.[31] All states also have state legislatures composed of elected representatives, and every state legislature, except one, is bicameral like the United States Congress.[32] The states' judicial branch is generally headed by that state's highest court with state judges, depending on the state, being either elected or appointed. Elected judges differ from the federal model where all federal judges are appointed by the President and confirmed by the Senate.[33]

18. The local governments in the United States are two-tiered: counties (also known as boroughs in Alaska and parishes in Louisiana) and municipalities (or cities and towns).[34] The governance structure of local governments is largely determined by that particular state's constitution.[35] Local governing bodies are, like federal and state governing bodies, generally elected by the people they serve.[36] Unlike state and federal governments, however, which share numerous powers, local governments derive their governing power only from specific grants by their specific state.[37] In other words, while states are co-sovereigns with the federal government, local governments do not share sovereignty with their states.

IV. Economic and Social Values[38]

19. The United States possesses the "largest and most technologically powerful national economy" of any country in the world. The primary long-term economic concerns of the United States have consistently been "inadequate investment in economic infrastructure, rapidly rising medical and pension costs of an aging population, sizable trade and budget deficits, and stagnation of family income in the lower economic groups."

20. The United States has the third-largest labor force in the world with 160 million workers, including those presently unemployed. Thirty-five and a half percent of the workforce is composed of those in managerial, professional, and technical fields; 24% in sales and office fields; 20% in manufacturing, extraction, transportation, and crafts fields; and the remainder in farming, forestry, fishing, and other service professions. The United States is the world's leading industrial power and

30. *Ibid.*
31. *Ibid.*
32. *Ibid.*
33. *Ibid.*; *see also* F. Klein, *Federal and State Court Systems: A Guide* 167 (Ballinger Publishing Co. 1977).
34. The White House, *Our Government: State and Local Government*, www.whitehouse.gov/ our_government/state_and_local_government/ (Jun. 8, 2009).
35. The White House, *Our Government: State and Local Government*, www.whitehouse.gov/ our_government/state_and_local_government/ (Jun. 8, 2009).
36. *Ibid.*
37. *Ibid.*
38. United States Central Intelligence Agency, *World Factbook: United States*, www.cia.gov/ library/ publications/the-world-factbook/geos/US.html (Oct. 25, 2019).

maintains a technologically advanced and highly diversified market, primarily in the industries of petroleum, steel, motor vehicles, aerospace, chemicals, food processing, lumber, consumer goods, mining, telecommunications, electronics, and aerospace. The country's main agricultural focuses are on vegetables, cotton, beef, poultry, pork, dairy products, wheat, corn, other grains, fish, and forest products.

The United States' Gross Domestic Product (GDP) in 2017 was the second largest in the world at an estimated USD 19 trillion, with a per capita GDP of USD 59,800. The United States is the largest importer in the world, importing an estimated USD 2.3 trillion in 2017, while exporting USD 1.55 trillion in 2017, making it the second-largest exporter in the world. The United States is also the largest importer and consumer of oil, the largest importer and consumer of natural gas, and the largest producer and consumer of electricity in the world. As a result of its high consumption and spending practices, the United States additionally possesses the greatest external debt of any country in the world, at USD 18 trillion as of March 2016.

§2. Legal Systems

I. Primacy of Legislation and Codification[39]

21. The Constitution is the highest law in the land, followed by legislation and treaties, and finally judicial opinions. Under the express provisions of Article III of the Constitution, the United States federal judiciary must decide the cases before it primarily in accordance with the Constitution and treaties, and secondarily in accordance with federal laws that do not conflict with the Constitution. The founders of the United States possessed an antipathy to codification of its laws and prior to the Constitution, the individual colonies had developed an extensive common-law system where the law is found in written judicial opinion rather than in a code. As a result, judicial precedents are the primary method of judicial decision-making in all states except Louisiana.[40] In addition, the current United States Code, while ultimately more binding on a court than a court's own prior decisions, is primarily codified as a result of judicial decisions that have been made over time on the various legal issues courts have decided.[41] A statute that does not violate the Constitution is more authoritative than a judicial opinion to the contrary, and in any event, the legislature may pass laws that overturn judicial opinions. The only judicial opinions that cannot be overturned by statute are those that deal with Constitutional law, as expressed by the Supreme Court of the United States.

39. L. Epstein & T. Walker, *Constitutional Law for a Changing America* 56–57 (6th ed., CQ Press 2007).
40. *Ibid.*
41. *Ibid.*

II. Position of the Judiciary

22. The United States maintains a dual judiciary system, composed of both state and federal courts. The federal judiciary cannot venture into the purview of the state courts and is only empowered to hear cases that fall within federal jurisdiction as set forth by Article III of the Constitution or by subsequent Congressional Acts.[42] The federal judiciary is composed of a Supreme Court, thirteen circuit Courts of Appeals, bankruptcy courts, and ninety-four district courts, including territorial courts in Puerto Rico, the United States Virgin Islands, Guam, and the Northern Mariana Islands.[43]

The Constitution gives federal courts, which are courts of limited jurisdiction, authority to hear cases that arise under the United States Constitution, the laws of the United States, or treaties; cases involving ambassadors; cases of maritime jurisdiction; controversies in which the United States is a party; controversies between two or more states, between a state and citizens of another state, between citizens of different states, or between a state or its citizens and citizens of foreign states.[44] The Supreme Court primarily exercises appellate jurisdiction, with the Court deciding for itself most of the cases it will hear, often limiting its docket to less than one hundred cases a year. The Court's discretionary docket generally involves cases of significant importance or cases where there is a split among the circuit Courts of Appeal.

23. The Constitution requires the trials of all crimes to be tried by juries held in the state in which the crime is alleged to have been committed.[45] Civil trials in which the amount in controversy exceeds USD 20 are also entitled to a jury trial.[46] In addition, in either a civil or criminal case, after a jury makes a determination of fact, an appellate court on review cannot reexamine that factual determination.[47] Although not mentioned in the Constitution, the courts also possess the power to review a law in relation to the United States Constitution and to declare the law unconstitutional and therefore void.[48]

24. The federal Courts of Appeals are the intermediary appellate courts below the Supreme Court and were created in 1891 to assist the Supreme Court with its appellate workload.[49] These courts have authority to review all final decisions made

42. R. Weise & A. de Grazia, *Eight Branches: American Government Today* 318 (Collegiate Publishing 1975).
43. Administrative Office of the United States Courts, *Frequently Asked Questions: Federal Judges*, www.uscourts.gov/faq.html (Jun. 3, 2009).
44. U.S. Const. Art. III, §2, cl. 1.
45. *Ibid.*, §2, cl. 3.
46. U.S. Const. Amend. VII.
47. *Ibid.*
48. *See Marbury v. Madison*, 5 U.S. 137, 180 (1803) (in which Justice Marshall wrote "the particular phraseology of the constitution of the United States confirms and strengthens the principle, supposed to be essential to all written constitutions, that a law repugnant to the constitution is void; and that courts, as well as other departments, are bound by that instrument").
49. F. Klein, *Federal and State Court Systems: A Guide* 172 (Ballinger Publishing Co. 1977).

by the district courts.[50] The federal Courts of Appeals also possess the power to review decisions by the administrative courts, which were created to enforce the orders of federal administrative agencies.[51]

25. The ninety-four district courts in the United States make up the federal trial courts.[52] All states have at least one district court, and the most populated states (Texas, New York, and California) each have four.[53] In addition, the United States also maintains district courts in the District of Columbia, the Northern Mariana Islands, Guam, Puerto Rico, and the United States Virgin Islands.[54] The district courts within the United States have exclusive jurisdiction over admiralty and maritime cases; seizures on land or water that are not within admiralty or maritime jurisdiction; proceedings against consuls or vice-consuls of other states; cases involving a fine, penalty, or forfeiture under federal law; and cases arising under patent or copyright laws.[55] Aside from these specific cases, the federal district courts share concurrent jurisdiction with state courts when the legal issue involves a federal question or a dispute of more than USD 75,000 and when the dispute involves citizens from different states.[56]

26. In addition to the Article III judiciary, the United States maintains a system of quasi-judicial legislative courts (i.e., administrative courts), which Congress has established for the specific purpose of carrying out one of the powers delegated to it by the Constitution.[57] Some examples include the territorial courts, the Court of Claims, the Customs Court, the Court of Military Appeals, and the Tax Courts. These courts are not created under Article III and therefore do not have as much judicial power because they were created and are controlled by legislative authority.[58]

27. Separate from the federal judiciary is the state judiciary, with every state maintaining its own state court system. All states have a judicial system that is similar to that of the federal judiciary, in that there are lower and appellate courts within each state. The highest reviewing court in a state, by whatever name it is called, is the ultimate reviewing authority over matters involving the interpretation of that state's constitution, statutes, and common law. Most states allow for the direct election of judges while others appoint judges through a process controlled by the legislature. There is minimal uniformity among states with regard to the jurisdiction of their intermediate appellate courts. All states with intermediate appellate courts also provide some means of discretionary review by the high court in that state.

---

50. *Ibid.*
51. *Ibid.*
52. *Ibid.*, 179.
53. *Ibid.*
54. *Ibid.*
55. *Ibid.*, 180.
56. *Ibid.*, 180–181.
57. R. Weise & A. de Grazia, *Eight Branches: American Government Today* 327–328 (Collegiate Publishing 1975).
58. F. Klein, *Federal and State Court Systems: A Guide* 180 (Ballinger Publishing Co. 1977).

III. Distinction Between Public and Private Law[59]

28. In the United States, public law—the law between government and individuals—is largely statutory while private law—the law dealing with individuals and their issues—is largely derived from judicial precedent. Generally, examples of fields of private law in the United States are torts and contracts, while examples of fields of public law are constitutional and administrative law. Traditionally, public law disputes have involved "more parties, more flexible relief, and more judicial initiative" than private law disputes, and the government is usually a party in public law litigation. These distinctions between private and public law historically were deeply grounded in a jurisprudence that sought to separate the two areas based on the concept of "an autonomous private order … designed to protect" certain individual property and personal rights. As such, private law developed as "that part of the legal system protecting the private ordering; [while] public law consisted of government compulsions restricting private freedom." Most modern fields of American law, however, are not grounded completely in public or private rules of law but, rather, contain some rules from each area.

IV. Sources of Private Law in General and of Tort Law in Particular

29. Historically, the private law system in the United States developed out of the English common-law system. No state in the United States, with the exception of Louisiana (a former French colony that has retained its Napoleonic code tradition), has completely codified its private law. Rather, the private law system is based on rules and principles that have developed over time through judicial decisions dating back 600 years. One advantage of the common-law system is its flexibility. Common law "may be changed, modified, or even overruled, where [old law does] not meet existing conditions."[60] As such, strict adherence to precedent is not practiced in many common-law matters. For example, tort principles have changed in the United States over the last few hundred years as society has changed.

Legislation has only slightly affected common-law torts in the United States, with the primary source of private law remaining judicial precedent. Courts often, however, draw guidance from state constitutional provisions that entitle citizens to remedies for wrongs sustained, even in the absence of specific legislation or judicial precedent addressing the particular wrong proven in a given case. With regard to tort law in the United States, common law is the primary source of tort jurisprudence. In the tort field, the American Law Institute, a private nonprofit organization, has been influential in shaping tort law by publishing Restatements of Law—works that restate the common law and also include suggested improvements that state courts can choose to adopt by judicial opinion. This monograph will occasionally cite the Restatement Second of Torts, but not often because the Restatement regularly fails to restate the common law and instead provides what the drafters of the

59. D. Farber & P. Frickey, *In the Shadow of the Legislature: The Common Law in the Age of the New Public Law*, Mich. L. Rev. 89, 885–886 (1991).
60. *Ibid.*

Restatement Second of Torts hoped the law would become—an unfortunate departure from the American Law Institute's original goal of providing a single source for the Restatement of the common law in the United States.

V. Law Used in This Monograph

30. Tort law is almost exclusively governed by the common law (i.e., judge-made law) of each state and there is no single statement of law that applies nationwide. Almost every tort found in this monograph will be found in every state, but each state has defined that tort in a non-uniform manner. In a number of areas, the law varies significantly from state to state, such as products liability. This monograph will provide the reader with the rule adopted in a majority of states as well as some rules adopted in a significant minority of states. Therefore, quotations from cases and treatises are provided to help the reader understand the general principles of American tort law. But these quoted sources should not be relied upon as the definitive statement for American tort law—for a definitive statement of tort law one must look to the laws of the fifty states, the District of Columbia, Puerto Rico, and the territories.

For some torts, there is widespread agreement among every state, but even for those torts, there may be a few states that have differing rules. This occurs because the common law is dynamic and tort law usually changes only after litigation. Thus, if a legal issue has not been litigated in seventy-five years then the law in that state reflects the thinking from the last time that issue was litigated, even though it is likely that a court looking at the same issue today would rule differently. For example, almost every American jurisdiction recognizes strict products liability, but a small number still do not. This can be explained by the fact that many states, beginning with California, began adopting strict products liability in the 1950s and some state courts have chosen not to adopt this new approach, instead relying on the traditional pre-1950 approaches to products liability. Because of this lack of uniformity, the best that this monograph can do is to provide the reader with a general understanding of an approach to American tort law, with the reader taking notice that a client in a particular state may be subject to a rule at variance with this monograph.

Two areas of law that will not be discussed in this monograph are worker's compensation and admiralty. Worker's compensation is a state-mandated insurance system that applies to most people in the workplace. It has its own set of rules that features what is basically a no-fault recovery system, bypassing the tort system except in a few cases of extreme employer misconduct. Admiralty law is governed by federal law and generally applies on the ocean and in navigable waterways, thus torts that occur on many rivers and lakes might be subject to admiralty jurisdiction and not state tort law.

§3. Function of the Law of Torts

I. Compensation

31. The primary purpose of United States tort law has been indemnification "against certain forms of harm to person, reputation, or estate, at the hands of [one's] neighbors, not because they are wrong, but because they are harms."[61] If a person knows that harm to another person will follow as a result of his or her act and commits the act anyway, resulting in harm to the other person, then he or she has committed a wrongful act for which the harmed person should be indemnified.[62] This is the signature principle of United States tort law.

II. Deterrence

32. Another important purpose of tort law is deterrence, which is meant to prevent tortfeasors from continuing certain acts that cause harm to others. Under this concept, an award of damages is not merely to compensate the person injured by the harm, but also to deter the wrongdoer from repeating the harm, as well as to serve as an example for other potential wrongdoers.

III. Punishment

33. A third purpose of tort law in the United States is punitive in nature and is designed to hold tortfeasors accountable for their tortious harms. This purpose is consistent with the tort principle of social responsibility and allocation of the cost of harm to the party responsible for causing the harm, whether negligently, recklessly, or intentionally. This retributive purpose is also consistent with the tort principle that the defendant should not just be deterred from such misconduct in the future but should actually be punished for having committed the tort in the first place. In practice, however, punitive damages are rare and generally assessed only when a tortfeasor's conduct is especially egregious, coupled with malice. Malice is generally established when a tortfeasor acts in reckless disregard for the rights of another or has some kind of evil motive. Ultimately, the inquiry for assessing punitive damages in a tort claim rests on whether the tortfeasor's conduct was such that it merits punishment beyond payment of compensation to the injured party.

61. O. Holmes, Jr., *The Common Law* 144 (Little, Brown, and Co. 1881).
62. *Ibid.*, 162.

§4. Relationship Between Tort and Criminal Law

I. Public Versus Private Wrongs

34. The relationship between tort and criminal law is based largely on the wrongs that each type of law addresses. Both tort law and criminal law seek to deter acts that society agrees are undesirable, but each type of law has a different ultimate purpose. Criminal law is directed at vindicating public wrongs, wrongs that an actor has made against society at large by violating the provisions of its criminal code. Tort law, on the other hand, is directed at righting private wrongs, wrongs that an actor has directed toward an individual victim by committing an act that, while not unlawful against society at large, is an act that is regarded as wrongful as to that specific person. An act can be a crime, a tort, or both; however, crimes are prosecuted by the government while torts are brought by those harmed by the tortfeasor.

35. The United States inherited the legal system of England, which in the Middle Ages did not recognize the sharp distinction made today between crime and tort. English judges and lawyers, ever so slowly, perceived that criminal and civil punishments served separate ultimate purposes, leading to the development, not of a separate codified civil law system, but a judge-made system of law for civil wrongs and their related remedies.

II. Differences in Punishments and Punishment Purposes

36. Although criminal and tort law are separate bodies of law in the United States, they also share many common characteristics. A single act may be both a tort and a crime. Whether the state chooses to prosecute the crime does not affect the individual victim's ability to pursue civil recovery for the tort. Civil courts, however, may take notice of whether a tortious act is also a crime in assessing whether it constitutes a tort. Criminal courts, on the other hand, will not define a tort as a crime just because it is tortious; rather, to be a crime, the conduct must fit the statutory or common-law definition of a particular crime.

While sharing some common traits, tort and criminal law have several differences. First, tort and criminal law differ procedurally. The government begins a criminal proceeding, whereas a tort victim institutes a civil action. The standards of proof in criminal and tort law also vary. In a criminal case, the burden of proof is that the state must prove all elements of the charged crime beyond a reasonable doubt. In tort, the victim must prove each of the elements of the tort by a preponderance of the evidence. Second, tort and criminal law differ with regard to the element of intent. Intent is the keystone element in assessing criminal liability, whereas a person can commit a tort even without the intent to do so, as in cases of negligence or strict liability. A third difference between tort and criminal law is the concept of harm. The government does not have to prove that a harm occurred if the act violates a criminal statute, whereas an essential element of a tort action is that a harm resulted from wrongful conduct.

§5. Relationship Between Contractual and Delictual or Tortious Responsibility

I. Statutory Distinctions: La Regle De Non Cumul

37. Tort and contract law in the United States are significantly different areas of law. Both areas developed largely through the common-law system, but contract law is premised on the notion that two or more individuals have the right to enter into any lawful agreement while tort law is based on righting the wrongs committed against someone.[63] Today, tort law is still primarily governed by the common law, while much of contract law has been codified through the adoption of the Uniform Commercial Code in forty-nine of the fifty states. The duty that arises from a contract is derived from the private agreement between the parties, whereas a wrong in tort is derived from a statute or case law making certain acts tortious. In addition, differences exist between the applicable statutes of limitations, recoverable damages, claim assignability, governmental immunities, and third-party liability.

Despite their many differences, "tort and contract concepts are not wholly discrete, however, and the same facts may give rise to liability under both."[64] There are some factual situations "where the lines of distinction [between tort and contract law] are shadowy and obscure, and the tort and the contract so approach each other, and become so nearly coincident as to make their practical separation somewhat difficult."[65] Since the common law in the United States does not recognize a strict dividing line between what actions fall under contract law and what actions fall under tort law, aggrieved parties often file actions under both areas of law for a single harm. Courts often, however, will look to see if the essence of an action lies in one particular area over the other, in determining which rules should apply (especially when determining the appropriate statutes of limitation and available remedies).

Even though contracts are largely governed by the agreement of the contracting parties, these agreements only govern because the law generally enforces the agreements into which people voluntarily enter. As such, both contract and tort law are governed by rules of law. In addition, contracts can also impose tort liability on the contracting parties, so that a tort arises when an injury occurs based on a contractual provision stating as much. Finally, tort law can, in limited circumstances, be used to overturn a contract when one of the contracting parties has committed a wrong. Some of these business torts include intentional interference with contracts and intentional interference with prospective business dealings.

---

63. *See Baratta v. Kozlowski*, 464 N.Y.S.2d 803, 807 (N.Y. App. Div. 1983).
64. *Victorson v. Bock Laundry*, 373 N.Y.S.2d 39 (N.Y. App. Div. 1975).
65. *Baratta v. Kozlowski*, 464 N.Y.S.2d 803, 807 (N.Y. App. Div. 1983).

II. Differences in Burdens of Proof

38. Despite the many differences between tort and contract law, these bodies of law share a common burden of proof at trial, which is often referred to as the "preponderance of the evidence" standard or the "more likely than not" standard. In mathematical terms, this standard is thought of as one side needing to convince the fact finder by more than 50%. The plaintiff is assigned the burden of proving each element of the tort or contract, while the defendant is assigned the burden of proving any affirmative defenses.

III. Differences in Remedies

39. Contract and tort law provide different remedies for the parties involved. For this reason, parties often allege contract and tort actions in order to obtain the best available remedy. The economic loss rule prevents such an election when the parties have a contractual connection with one another and when the only harm sustained is economic. In such a situation, the economic loss rule "prohibits plaintiffs from recovering in tort economic losses to which their entitlement flows only from contract because tort law is not intended to compensate parties for losses suffered as a result of a breach of duties assumed only by agreement."[66] "Tort law … is concerned with the obligations imposed by law, rather than by bargain … [whereas contract law] protects expectation interests, and provides an appropriate set of rules when an individual bargains for a product of particular quality or for a particular use."[67] Probably the most significant difference between the two is the availability of punitive damages in tort.

40. The economic loss rule serves to maintain these fundamental differences between tort and contract law. In summary:

> the economic loss rule bars "recovery for alleged breach of tort duties where a contractual relationship exists and the losses are economic losses. If the economic loss rule applies, the party will be held to contract remedies, regardless of how the plaintiff characterizes the claims …. The key inquiry is the nature of the loss and the manner in which it occurs, i.e., are the losses economic losses, with economic losses distinguished from personal injury or injury to other property. If the claimed loss is an economic loss, and no exception applies to the economic loss rule, then the parties will be limited to contractual remedies."[68]

66. *Alejandre v. Bull*, 153 P.3d 864, 868 (Wash. 2007) (citing *Factory Mkt., Inc. v. Schuller Int'l, Inc.*, 987 F.Supp. 387, 395 (E.D. Pa. 1997)).
67. *Alejandre*, 153 P.3d, at 868 (citing *Stuart v. Coldwell Banker Commercial Group, Inc.*, 745 P.2d 1284 (Wash. 1987)).
68. *Ibid.*, 158 P.3d, 868–869.

§6. Protected Interests

41. The United States tort system seeks to provide compensation to those who have sustained injuries due to the fault of others in certain areas, where American tort law has decided redress should be provided. Historically, the interests that tort law seeks to redress are an individual's interest in life and health, liberty and bodily integrity, property and economic loss, and reputation and privacy.

I. Life and Health

42. While American tort law serves to protect a variety of interests, it provides the greatest legal protection to the interests of physical security in one's person and property. Within that protected category, the highest level of protection is afforded to one's life and health. Several torts exist to remedy the interference with a person's life and health, including the intentional torts of assault and battery, as well as other torts to the person based on negligence principles and strict liability torts for harms caused by dangerous animals, abnormally dangerous activities, or defective products.

II. Liberty and Bodily Integrity

43. As mentioned above, American tort law seeks to protect an individual's interest in his person, which includes the interests of liberty (freedom from restraint) and bodily integrity (personal autonomy). Intentional and negligent interference with these interests is almost always tortious absent a recognized justification. Examples of torts involving these interests include intentional torts of battery, assault, false imprisonment, trespass to chattels, trespass to real property, and conversion, as well as other torts grounded in negligence principles. Commission of a tort against a person or his property exposes the tortfeasor to all damages that are reasonably related to the tort, including potentially punitive damages depending on the egregiousness of the act.

III. Property and Economic Loss

44. Although an individual's rights in property are highly regarded under American tort law, the courts are reluctant to impose liability in tort for purely economic harm, as the appropriate remedy in such a case is often found in contract law. Certain interferences with economic interests, however, may result in tort liability, although, as a general rule, courts are more cautious in imposing tort liability absent some physical interference. Potential torts against economic interests are intentional interference with contract or economic opportunity, negligent interference with contract or economic interests, unfair competition, nuisance, misrepresentation, nondisclosure, trespass and conversion.

IV. Reputation and Privacy

45. American tort law offers certain protection to one's emotional security and other intangible interests, although the courts are more hesitant to assess tort liability in such cases. Some interferences with a person's intangible interests are tortious, while others are not. Absent some physical interference with a person or his property, courts exercise extreme caution in imposing liability for intangible harm only. That being said, the United States tort system does provide remedies for certain harms to intangible interests, such as can be found in the torts of intentional infliction of emotional distress, negligent infliction of emotional distress, defamation, invasion of privacy, abuse of process, loss of consortium, and alienation of affection.

Part I. Liability for One's Own Acts

Chapter 1. General Principles

§1. Unlawfulness and Fault

46. "Unlawfulness" is not required for tort recovery because of the sharp distinction between criminal liability and civil liability, with unlawfulness viewed as criminal conduct. While almost all criminal (i.e., "unlawful") conduct may result in a tort, not all tortious conduct is criminal conduct. While older case law often referred to certain tortious conduct as unlawful, most courts have abandoned that language. Today all torts are classified under one of three bases of liability: intent, negligence, or strict liability.

I. Intent

47. The law of intentional torts basically follows Aristotle's formulation: an intentional wrong, causing harm, and without consent of the victim.[69] Intentional torts require that a person know that he committed a specific act, though the actor does not necessarily have to know that the act is wrongful. Intentional torts examine what a person knew at the time they committed an act. Intent does not necessarily imply wrongdoing and is never, without an act, a tort on its own. Whether an intentional act becomes tortious depends on the elements of a specific intentional tort. In addition, the intent "with which tort liability is concerned is not necessarily a hostile intent, or desire to do any harm. Rather it is an intent to bring about a result which will invade the interest of another in a way that the law forbids."[70] This intent does not necessarily examine the motive for the act but rather the intentional commission of the act itself that, even if performed as a good-natured joke or for the benefit of the plaintiff, may be tortious if that act itself is a tort.[71] In other words, motive without the requisite intent is insufficient to establish an intentional tort. But motive can be probative evidence considered by the fact finder in inferring intent.

69. Aristotle, *Rhetoric* bk. I, Ch. 13 (Cambridge University Press 1909).
70. *Farmers and Mechs. Mut. Ins. Co. of West Virginia v. Cook*, 557 S.E.2d 801, 809 (W. Va. 2001) (citing W. Keeton et al., *Prosser & Keeton on Torts* §8, 36 (5th ed., West Publishing 1984)).
71. *Ibid.*

48. The intent is established by looking at what the tortfeasor knew and not what they should have known. However, recklessness—the conscious disregard for the rights of others that creates a substantial risk of harm—often serves as a substitute for intent for many intentional torts. Recklessness is something more than ordinary negligence and is sometimes referred to as gross negligence. The Restatement explains:

> Recklessness may consist of either of two different types of conduct. In one the actor knows, or has reason to know … of facts which create a high degree of risk of physical harm to another, and deliberately proceeds to act, or to fail to act, in conscious disregard of, or indifference to, that risk. In the other the actor has such knowledge, or reason to know, of the facts, but does not realize or appreciate the high degree of risk involved, although a reasonable man in his position would do so. An objective standard is applied to him, and he is held to the realization of the aggravated risk which a reasonable man in his place would have, although he does not himself have it.[72]

II. Negligence (Fault)

49. Tort liability in negligence is premised on the notion that people are required to act reasonably under all circumstances to those to whom they owe a duty of care. Generally, an individual owes a duty to every other individual "to use reasonable care to avoid injury to the other person in any situation in which it could be reasonably anticipated or foreseen that a failure to use such care might result in such injury."[73] Courts look at many factors in determining whether a duty exists in a particular fact situation, such as the following:

> The foreseeability of harm to the plaintiff, the degree of certainty that the plaintiff suffered injury, the closeness of the connection between the defendant's conduct and the injury suffered, the moral blame attached to the defendant's conduct, the policy of preventing future harm, the extent of the burden to the defendant and consequences to the community of imposing a duty to exercise care with resulting liability for breach, and the availability, cost, and prevalence of insurance for the risk involved.[74]

The term "gross negligence" is occasionally used by the courts, but it is not used consistently across the United States. In some states, it is used as a substitute for recklessness, while at other times gross negligence is defined as extremely negligent conduct—falling somewhere between ordinary negligence and recklessness. In

72. Restatement (Second) of Torts §500 cmt. a (1965).

73. *Baccus v. Ameripride Srvcs, Inc.*, 179 P.3d 309, 312 (Idaho 2008) (citing *Coghlan v. Beta Theta Pi Fraternity*, 987 P.2d 300, 311 (Idaho 1999)).

74. *Ibid.*

some states, the term is used inconsistently in that state, with one definition controlling one area of law and an alternate definition used in a different area. Regardless of how it is defined, gross negligence differs from ordinary negligence in degree and not in kind—its focus is still on the wrongdoer's conduct.

III. Strict Liability

50. Strict liability focuses on the activity the tortfeasor was engaged in rather than the tortfeasor's conduct (i.e., what the tortfeasor knew or should have known). It is irrelevant under strict liability that the tortfeasor was acting reasonably or that the tortfeasor exercised the highest level of care. The law has classified certain activities (e.g., owning wild animals, manufacturing dangerous products, or engaging in ultra-hazardous activities) as falling under strict liability, so the first issue in any strict liability action is whether the tortfeasor was engaged in one of the defined activities.

§2. Concept of Fault

51. Arguably all tort cases involve some type of moral fault or guilt, but fault, in the legal sense, is closely identified with the tort of negligence. Many cases often refer to negligence and fault interchangeably, with negligence defined as duty and breach of that duty. In other words, a person is at fault when they breach their duty of care by acting unreasonably under the circumstances. But proving fault is not the same as proving a negligence cause of action, which, in addition to fault, requires that the plaintiff establish actual cause, proximate cause, and harm.

§3. Duty of Care

52. A person that owes a duty to another is required to conform to a specified standard of care. Generally, the standard of care is determined in one of several ways: (1) the default rule is that one has a "duty to act as a reasonably prudent person under similar circumstances;" (2) the standard may be created by a civil tort statute; (3) the standard may be created by a criminal statute through the negligence per se doctrine; or[75] (4) the status of the wrongdoer can establish the standard of care. Courts decide "the nature of the duty, and the specific persons to whom it is owed" based on the specific facts of a particular case.[76] The fact finder, usually a jury, determines whether the defendant's conduct has fallen below the applicable standard of care.

---

75. *Allen v. Cox*, 942 A.2d 296, 300 (Conn. 2008) (citing *Lodge v. Arett Sales Corp.*, 717 A.2d 215 (Conn. 1998); *Jaworski v. Kiernan*, 696 A.2d 332 (Conn. 1997)).
76. *Ibid.*

I. General Standard: Reasonably Prudent Person

A. *Overview*

53. Absent a statute imposing a different duty as mentioned above, the general default duty that citizens owe to one another is that of a reasonable person, which is to exercise ordinary care under the circumstances. Ordinary care under the circumstances means exercising the same level of care that a reasonable and prudent person would exercise under the same or similar circumstances to avoid harming another person.[77] This reasonable person is an adult with average knowledge and skills of someone that lives in the community where the injury occurred. The standard is primarily objective, with some subjective considerations. Specifically:

> The reasonably prudent person standard "reflects the community's demand for a standard that is external and objective. To be complete, however, a standard of care must also be subjective, in that it makes proper allowance for the actor's capacity to meet the risk apparent to him, and the circumstances under which he must act. Accordingly, the basic reasonable person standard allows for and incorporates the physical characteristics of the defendant, himself. Other 'circumstances' may be similarly incorporated into the reasonable person standard."[78]

B. *Malfeasance, Nonfeasance, and No Duty to Act*

54. It is well established that the law, under most circumstances, does not impose a duty on people for failing to act. For example, a stranger that can easily throw a life preserver toward a drowning victim is not required to do so, and the stranger that lets a drowning victim die has not committed a tort. Generally speaking, the law requires individuals "to refrain from engaging in misfeasance, affirmative acts that a reasonable person 'should recognize as involving an unreasonable risk of causing an invasion of an interest of another' or acts 'which involve[] an unreasonable risk of harm to another.'"[79] Nonfeasance occurs when someone with a duty to act fails to do so—the omission is actionable, though breach of duty must still be established. In this situation, the plaintiff must prove there was a "special relationship … between the parties such that social policy justifies the imposition of a duty to act."[80] Examples include a parent-child relationship and companions out on a common undertaking.

---

77. *Mansfield v. Circle K Corp.*, 87 P.2d 1130, 1132 (Okla. 1994).
78. *Advincula v. United Blood Srvcs.*, 678 N.E.2d 1009, 1020 (Ill. 1996) (citing W. Keeton et al., *Prosser & Keeton on Torts* §32 (6th ed., West Publishing 1995)).
79. *Giggers v. Memphis Hous. Auth.*, 277 S.W.3d 359, 364 (Tenn. 2009) (quoting Restatement (Second) of Torts §§284, 302 (1965); W. Keeton et al., *supra* n. 70, at §56, 373).
80. W. Keeton et al., *supra* n. 70, at §56, 373.

C. Who Owes a Duty of Care (Foreseeability)

55. The question of who owes a duty of care is significant because if no duty is owed, there is no negligence. The Connecticut Supreme Court explained:

> Although it has been said that no universal test for [duty] ever has been formulated …, our threshold inquiry has always been whether the specific harm alleged by the plaintiff was foreseeable to the defendant. The ultimate test of the existence of the duty to use care is found in the foreseeability that harm may result if it is not exercised …. By that is not meant that one charged with negligence must be found actually to have foreseen the probability of harm or that the particular injury which resulted was foreseeable, but the test is, would the ordinary [person] in the defendant's position, knowing what he knew or should have known, anticipate that harm of the general nature of that suffered was likely to result?[81]

56. Judges have the responsibility to determine whether a person owes a legal duty to another because the initial question of whether a duty is owed is a question of law and not fact. This is important because in the United States issues of fact are decided by juries, and thus a decision by a judge that no duty was owed bypasses the jury process. At one time most courts discussed the foreseeability issue under duty and were able to take many cases away from the jury. Today most courts place foreseeability issues under proximate cause, thus giving juries the ability to determine whether a person was the proximate cause of the injury. Though judges still have the power to determine who owes a duty, in practice, the duty question will only be decided by the judge in cases where it is clear that no duty was owed. For example, a judge should have no difficulty in deciding that a stranger owed no duty to a stranded motorist they saw on the road.

D. Duty to Rescue

57. Because there is no legal duty to act there is likewise no legal duty to rescue, "and absent a special relationship, the law imposes no duty to act affirmatively to protect someone from danger unless the dangerous situation was created by the defendant."[82] Morally, a stranger may have a responsibility to help a lost child in the forest, but there is no legal duty to assist the child. Thus, a lawsuit against the stranger by the lost child's parents will be dismissed.

58. But in some cases a person may form a special relationship with another, thereby creating an affirmative duty to act. "[I]f an individual stands in a special

81. *Allen v. Cox*, 285 Conn. 603, 610, 942 A.2d 296, 300 (Conn. 2008) (citing *Jaworski v. Kiernan*, 696 A.2d 332 (Conn. 1997)).

82. *Jackson v. Tedd-Lait Post No. 75, American Legion*, 723 A.2d 1220, 1221 (Me. 1999) (citing *Hughes v. Beta Upsilon Bldg. Ass'n*, 619 A.2d 525, 527 (Me. 1993); Restatement (Second) of Torts §314 (1965)).

relationship to another individual who is the source of the danger or who is foreseeably at risk from the danger, then the individual assumes an affirmative duty to exercise reasonable care to either control the danger or protect the vulnerable."[83] For example, an expert swimmer agrees to protect a friend when they go fishing. If the friend falls into a lake the swimmer has a legal duty to rescue his friend, or at least attempt a rescue, and failure to act will establish the swimmer's breach of duty. A second situation involves a person that creates a risk to others, such as accidentally letting a fire in the woods get out of control. In that situation, there would be a duty to warn others he sees in the woods about the fire heading in their direction.

Some special relationships are created by law and "include ... innkeeper and guest, common carrier and passenger, possessors of land and guests, social host and guest, and those who have custody over another."[84] The most common types of custodians comprise people that take care of children, prisoners, the mentally infirm, and the elderly.

59. Thankfully, most people do not think in terms of duty and they immediately begin to rescue a person in need. As Justice Cardozo, a noted jurist, said "[d]anger invites rescue. The cry of distress is the summons to relief."[85] But once a person chooses to act they must act reasonably under the circumstances. Suppose, for example, that a hiker falls off a cliff and calls for help. Stranger arrives, throws down a rope, and tells hiker to secure the rope around his waist. It would be unreasonable for stranger to then attach the rope to his automobile and accelerate to 100 kilometers per hour with the hiker attached to the rope. As the Minnesota Supreme Court explained:

> [O]ne has a duty to act when he "undertakes, gratuitously or for consideration, to render services to another which he should recognize as necessary for the protection of a third person or his things," and liability will be imposed if (1) his failure to act increases the risk of harm; (2) he undertook a duty owed by the other to the third party; or (3) the harm is suffered because the other or the third person relied on the undertaking.[86]

A duty is imposed on a rescuer when the rescuer begins to rescue and unreasonably stops before completing the rescue, resulting in others not coming to the victim's aid.

60. Some people are paid to rescue others, and thereby the law imposes on them an affirmative duty to act. The Ohio Court of Appeals explicated:

---

83. *Downs ex rel Downs v. Bush*, 263 S.W.3d 812, 819–820 (Tenn. 2008) (citing *West v. East Tenn. Pioneer Oil Co.*, 172 S.W.3d 545, 551 (Tenn. 2005); *Biscan v. Brown*, 160 S.W.3d 462, 478–479 (Tenn. 2005)).
84. *Downs ex rel Downs v. Bush*, 263 S.W.3d 812, 818 (Tenn. 2008) (citing Restatement (Second) of Torts §314A (1965)).
85. *Wagner v. Int'l Ry.*, 133 N.E. 437, 437 (N.Y. 1926).
86. *Bjerke v. Johnson*, 742 N.W.2d 660, 665 (Minn. 2007) (citing *Walsh v. Pagra Air Taxi, Inc.*, 282 N.W.2d 567, 571 (Minn. 1979); Restatement (Second) of Torts §324A (1965)).

> A duty of care may be imposed by operation of law or by contract. A contractual duty to act may be express or implied. When one undertakes a duty to perform an act, and another reasonably relies on that undertaking, the act must generally be performed with ordinary care. While a breach of contract is ordinarily not a tort, a common-law duty to perform with care, skill, reasonable expedience, and faithfulness is incidental to every contract, and the negligent failure to observe those conditions may constitute a tort. For a breach of that duty, a person injured as a proximate result has a right of action based on the contractor's failure to exercise due care in the performance of his assumed obligation.[87]

Swimming pool lifeguards are under a duty to rescue those in their pool and may not let someone drown if they can do so reasonably—there is no duty to die attempting a rescue.

E. Duty to Control and to Protect

61. Generally, there is no duty to control the conduct of another person to prevent that person from causing harm. However, when a person has "a special relationship with a person posing a risk," courts will recognize "a duty to control the conduct of another for the benefit of a third party in narrowly prescribed circumstances."[88] In one case, the court explained that the Department of Corrections and the state parole board had a special relationship with a released prisoner because of the amount of control the Department and the board exercised over the prisoner.[89] In addition, courts have recognized a duty to control a person when the duty is imposed by statute. In one situation, the court held a town liable to a person that was injured after a police officer released a drunk driver, who then caused an injury. In that instance, the officer had a duty to not let the drunk driver continue driving while under the influence of alcohol.[90]

62. Under the Second Restatement of Torts, if a person can prove a special relationship between the defendant and a third party who causes harm to the plaintiff:

> an action may be maintained against the defendant for negligent supervision liability in accordance with section 317 of the Restatement. Section 315(b) provides that there is a duty to control the conduct of a third person to prevent him from causing harm to another if "a special relation exists between the actor and the other which gives to the other a right to protection." If a special relationship exists pursuant to section 315(b), a plaintiff is then entitled to assert a claim for negligent supervision pursuant to section 317, which provides: A

87. *Hubbell v. Xenia*, 885 N.E.2d 290, 295 (Ohio Ct. App. 2008) (citations omitted).

88. *Leavitt v. Brockton Hosp., Inc.*, 907 N.E.2d 213, 216–217 (Mass. 2009) (citing *Jean W. v. Commonwealth*, 610 N.E.2d 305 (Mass. 1993) (Liacos, C.J., concurring)).

89. *Ibid.*

90. *Ibid.* (Mass. 2009) (citing *Irwin v. Ware*, 467 N.E.2d 1292 (Mass. 1984)).

> master is under a duty to exercise reasonable care so to control his servant while acting outside the scope of his employment as to prevent him from intentionally harming others or from so conducting himself as to create an unreasonable risk of bodily harm to them, if (a) the servant (i) is upon the premises in possession of the master or upon which the servant is privileged to enter only as his servant, or (ii) is using the chattel of the master, and (b) the master (i) knows or has reason to know that he has the ability to control his servant, and (ii) knows or should know of the necessity and opportunity for exercising such control ... Section 315(b) uses the term "special relation" in a narrower sense than it is traditionally used. A comment to section 315(b) expressly confines the term "special relation," ... to four kinds of relationships: (1) common carriers and their passengers; (2) innkeepers and their guests; (3) possessors of land and members of the public who are their invitees; and (4) those who are required by law to take physical custody of another or who voluntarily do so, such as to deprive the other of his normal opportunities for protection.[91]

Special relationships can be created in many ways as courts find new ways to impose a duty to act. In one case the court found that two social companions were in a special relationship when they talked to some women and followed them to a restaurant, resulting in one of them being severely beaten and the other failing to help the one who was beaten.[92]

63. Traditionally, landlords owed no duties to their tenants or their tenants' guests because property law—derived from feudal rights—conveyed all rights in the land from the landlord to the tenant. While not imposing tort duties on landlords renting thatch huts to villains made sense in the middle ages, that ancient rationale does not make much sense for modern apartment dwellers in New York City. The Michigan Supreme Court declared:

> Specifically in landlord and tenant law, this Court has stated that "a landlord may be held liable for an unreasonable risk of harm caused by a dangerous condition in the areas of common use retained in his control … ." The rationale behind imposing a duty to protect these special relationships is based on control. In each situation one person entrusts himself to the control and protection of another, with a consequent loss of control to protect himself. The duty to protect is imposed upon the person in control because he is best able to provide a place of safety … . Whether a common area is sufficiently safe to be fit for its intended purpose depends on the condition of the area in question.[93]

91. *Dragomir v. Spring Harbor Hosp.*, 970 A.2d 310, 315–316 (Me. 2009) (citing *Fortin v. Roman Catholic Bishop of Portland*, 871 A2d 1208, 1220–1222 (Me. 2009); Restatement (Second) of Torts §§314, 315(b), 317, 320 (1965)).
92. *Farwell v. Keaton*, 240 N.W.2d 217 (Mich. 1976).
93. *Allison v. AEW Capital Mgmt., L.L.P.*, 751 N.W.2d 8, 22 (Mich. 2008) (citing *Williams v. Cunningham Drug Stores, Inc.*, 418 N.W.2d 381 (Mich. 1988)).

In addition, landlords are liable for negligent repairs, dangerous conditions known to the landlord but not disclosed to the tenant, and for the landlord's contractual obligations to make repairs.

Another general rule is that a landowner has no duty to protect those on his property from the criminal acts of third parties who are not subject to the premises occupier's control. But as a Texas court explained:

> This rule "is not absolute; a person who occupies or controls premises has a duty to use ordinary care to protect invitees, including tenants, from criminal acts of third parties if he or she knows or has reason to know of an unreasonable and foreseeable risk of harm to the invitee. This duty is commensurate with the right of control over the property. Thus, a landlord owes such a duty to a tenant when the landlord has retained the right to control part of the leased premises."[94]

For example, when a landlord's property is in a high-crime area and there have been criminal assaults near the property, the landlord must take reasonable steps in protecting the property, such as repairing a broken intercom system that allows guests into the building or providing adequate lighting in the parking lot.

Negligently providing security to third parties is also a basis for liability. One court explained:

> [W]hile the owner of a business is not generally charged with a duty to protect customers from criminal acts by third parties, an intervening criminal act by a third party may not always release an owner from liability for negligence .... A possessor of land who holds it open to the public for entry for his business purposes is subject to liability to members of the public while they are upon the land for such a purpose, for physical harm caused by the accidental, negligent, or intentionally harmful acts of third persons or animals, and by the failure of the possessor to exercise reasonable care to (a) discover that such acts are being done or are likely to be done .... Since the possessor is not an insurer of the visitor's safety, he is ordinarily under no duty to exercise any care until he knows or has reason to know that the acts of the third person are occurring, or are about to occur .... If the place or character of his business, or his past experience, is such that he should reasonably anticipate careless or criminal conduct on the part of third persons, either generally or at some particular time, he may be under a duty to take precautions against it, and to provide a reasonably sufficient number of servants to afford a reasonable protection.[95]

64. The government has a duty to protect the public, but generally no duty to any one individual. Because of limited resources, the government is allowed to exercise broad discretion in allocating its resources. The government may voluntarily

---

94. *Durham v. Zarcades*, 270 S.W.3d 708, 712–713 (Tex. App. 2008) (citations omitted).

95. *Parks v. Characters Night Club*, 548 S.E.2d 605, 609–610 (S.C. Ct. App. 2001) (citing Restatement (Second) of Torts §344 and cmt. f (1965)).

assume a duty to protect those with whom it creates a special relationship. For example, if X calls the police to report a burglary while hiding under his bed, a special relationship is formed if the police say they are sending an officer to the house right away. Once that special relationship is formed, the police must act reasonably.

II. Statutory Standard

A. *Statutory Violation*

65. There are very few civil statutes that establish specific tort liability, with the vast majority of negligence cases decided through judicially established standards of care. In those rare circumstances where there is a civil tort statute, the statute establishes the standard of care and thus the duty owed, and a violation of the statute establishes the breach of that particular duty. Defendants that violate a statute are precluded from arguing that they nonetheless were acting reasonably under the circumstances because the civil statute is the substitute for the default rule of reasonable care. For example, it might be reasonable for a sporting event to have one security guard for every two-hundred spectators, but if the statute requires one security guard for every fifty spectators then that higher standard must be met or the organizer of the sporting event will be found to have breached the duty of care.

B. *Negligence Per Se*

66. The negligence per se doctrine allows a court to use a criminal statute, regulation, or ordinance as a substitute for the reasonably prudent person's standard of care. The courts may adopt this standard of care because it is assumed that a reasonably prudent person follows the law. The decision on whether to allow a litigant to use negligence per se is within the sound discretion of the trial judge.

When courts adopt a criminal statute for a negligence cause of action, the violation of the statute is said to be negligence per se. Negligence per se is a means of establishing the duty owed, and violation of the statute is said to establish a breach of that duty. But to prevail in the lawsuit, a litigant must also establish the other negligence elements: actual cause, proximate cause, and harm.

To establish negligence per se on the basis of a statutory violation the party must establish that: (1) the injury was caused by the violation; (2) the injury was of a type intended to be prevented by the statute; and (3) the injured party was in the class meant to be protected by the statute.[96]

67. Accidents involving traffic violations generally do not fall into the negligence per se category. Governments regulate who may drive, how fast they may drive, what they may drive, and many other aspects of driving. But when a person violates a traffic regulation courts rarely employ the negligence per se doctrine.

---

96. *Mansfield v. Circle K. Corp.*, 877 P.2d 1130, 1132–1133 (Okla. 1994) (citing *Miller v. City of Portland*, 288 Or. 271, 604 P.2d 1261, 1264 (Or. 1980)).

68. Courts alone decide whether to exercise their discretion in allowing or denying the use of negligence per se. If denied, the plaintiff may continue the litigation by using the general standard of care—what a reasonably prudent person would do under like circumstances. In most cases, the result under the general standard or negligence per se will be the same. The primary advantage of negligence per se is that it limits the jury's discretion. Under negligence per se, the jury is told what the standard is and their task is to determine whether the defendant violated the statute or ordinance. Contrast that to the general standard, where the jury must first determine what was reasonable and then whether the defendant was unreasonable.

69. Negligence per se is not used when children are accused of negligence and instead, the normal standard applicable to children is used. "It is the jury's role to determine whether the violation of a statute or ordinance by a child constitutes negligence considering his age, education, experience and intelligence."[97]

70. Even when negligence per se establishes the standard of care, violation of a statute is sometimes excused and therefore not negligence. Some common excuses include:

> (a) the violation is reasonable because of the actor's incapacity; (b) he neither knows nor should know of the occasion for compliance; (c) he is unable after reasonable diligence or care to comply; (d) he is confronted by an emergency not due to his own misconduct; (e) compliance would involve a greater risk of harm to the actor or to others. Under category (a), "incapacity," could come cases where the violator was too young, or did not have the mental capacity, to be charged with negligence. It might include a blind man who unknowingly walks a red light (though he may be contributorily negligent for other reasons), or a driver who is rendered physically incapable because of a heart attack. Under category (b) could come cases where a night driver has a tail light to go out unexpectedly and without his knowledge. Under category (c), "unable after reasonable diligence or care to comply," could come cases involving impossibility .... Under category (d), "emergency not due to his own misconduct," could come cases in which there is an unexpected failure in the steering or braking system; a blowout of a tire which is reasonably thought to be in good condition; a sudden confrontation with blinding dust or smoke on the highway. It could include driving on the left side of the highway to avoid striking a darting child, and similar situations. Finally, ... category (e), "greater risk of harm," is one in which the law requires people to walk facing traffic, but due to particular circumstances, it would involve greater risk to walk upon that side.[98]

While failure to comply with a statute usually results in negligence per se, the opposite is not true. Compliance with a statute is not a safe harbor from negligence,

97. *Bentley v. Stewart*, 594 N.E.2d 1061, 1063 (Ohio Ct. App. 1992).
98. *Impson v. Structural Metals, Inc.*, 487 S.W.2d 694 (Tex. 1972) (citing Restatement (Second) of Torts §288A (1965)).

though it is evidence of reasonable conduct. In other words, negligence per se can only be used as a sword by the plaintiff and not as a shield by the defendant. For example, a railroad company that is sued by a person injured at a railroad crossing cannot contend that the railroad was not negligent based on the railroad's full compliance with all laws regulating railroad crossings.

III. Landowners and Possessors

71. A majority of jurisdictions follow some form of the status approach in determining the duty landowners or land possessors owe to those that enter their land. At common law, an entrant on another person's land was either a trespasser, invitee, or licensee. The North Carolina Supreme Court explained:

> The highest degree of care a landowner owes is the duty of reasonable care toward those entrants classified as invitees. Specifically, a landowner owes an invitee a duty to use ordinary care to keep his property reasonably safe and to warn of hidden perils or unsafe conditions that could be discovered by reasonable inspection and supervision. A landowner's duty toward a licensee, on the other hand, is significantly less stringent. The duty of care owed to a licensee by an owner or possessor of land ordinarily is to refrain from doing the licensee willful injury and from wantonly and recklessly exposing him to danger. Thus, a licensee enters another's premises at his own risk and enjoys the license subject to its concomitant perils. Finally, with respect to trespassers, a landowner need only refrain from the willful or wanton infliction of injury. Willful injury constitutes actual knowledge of the danger combined with a design, purpose, or intent to do wrong and inflict injury. Similarly, a wanton act is performed intentionally with a reckless indifference to the injuries likely to result.[99]

Of the states that retain the status approach, very few recognize the licensee category. Thus the two status categories that remain are invitees (i.e., legal entrants to the land) and trespassers (i.e., illegal entrants to the land). A person's status on the land varies depending on the permission he has. The status may change depending on where he is on the land or if his permission to remain on the land has been revoked. For example, a store customer is an invitee when in the public areas of a store, but his status would change to trespasser when he enters an "employee only" section of the store.

72. An exception to the duty owed to legal entrants on the land is the open and obvious doctrine. Under this principle, "an occupier or owner of premises is under no duty to protect any person, including business invitees, against dangers that are so open and obvious that the 'nature of the hazard itself serves as a warning. Thus,

---

99. *Nelson v. Freeland*, 507 S.E.2d 882, 884 (N.C. 1998) (citations omitted).

the owner or occupier may reasonably expect that persons entering the premises will discover those dangers and take appropriate measures to protect themselves.'"[100]

73. Trespassing children are treated differently than trespassing adults under the attractive nuisance doctrine, also less commonly referred to as the turntable doctrine. The rule provides:

> [A] duty will be imposed on an owner, occupier or controller of land to remedy a dangerous condition on the premises or to otherwise protect children from injury resulting from it where (1) the owner, occupier or controller knew or should have known that children habitually frequent the property; (2) a defective structure or dangerous condition was present on the property; (3) the defective structure or dangerous condition was likely to injure children because they are incapable, because of age and maturity, of appreciating the risk involved; and (4) the expense and burden of remedying the defective structure or dangerous condition was slight when compared to the risk created to children.[101]

The attractive nuisance doctrine generally does not apply to naturally occurring conditions on the land, such as a lake, stream, or tree. Also, the attractive nuisance doctrine does not apply when a plaintiff is harmed by something that a child of similar age and experience should have appreciated.

74. Almost half of the fifty states have either partially or completely abolished the status approach and now apply the same standard used in other negligence cases: the reasonably prudent person under similar circumstances standard. Though the standard of care has changed, evidence concerning the relationship of the injured party to the land is still significant. For example, in a state that has completely abolished the status rules, it is relevant that the injured party was a trespasser. The primary practical effect in a state that has abolished the status rules is that more cases will survive a summary judgment motion to dismiss the case, thereby allowing more cases to reach the jury. Even so, it is difficult to imagine many cases that will reach different results. Presumably, a burglar that trips on a shoe left in an unlit hallway in a person's home would not recover from his injuries.

§4. Capacity (Infants, Minors, Other Incompetents)

I. Intentional Torts

75. A person's mental state is not a factor in determining whether that person committed an intentional tort. Intentional torts require that wrongdoers know that they are committing an act; therefore, motives and beliefs are generally irrelevant.

---

100. *Kirchner v. Shooters on the Water, Inc.*, 856 N.E.2d 1026, 1032 (Ohio Ct. App. 2006) (citing *Armstrong v. Best Buy Co., Inc.*, 788 N.E.2d 1088 (Ohio 2003)).
101. *Calhoun ex rel. Calhoun v. Belt Royal Co. of Chicago*, 731 N.E.2d 332, 337 (Ill. App. Ct. 2000).

For example, in one case, the wrongdoer believed he was a god, could fly, and was convinced that his son-in-law was an agent of a hostile foreign government. The court held that even though the wrongdoer was insane, he was liable for an intentional tort because he knew he was committing the act of shooting another person.[102]

76. Likewise, a child's age is not a bar to recovery from an intentional tort. "[M]inority, standing alone, is insufficient to establish as a matter of law that [a young child] lacked the requisite intent to commit a battery .... [T]here is currently no specific age at which minors are immune from liability for intentional torts as a matter of law."[103] However, age is probative, for the youngest of children, in determining if intent can be established. For example, it is likely impossible for a five-month-old infant to be capable of forming the intent necessary to create a tort. A few states still follow the rule of sevens, where a child seven or under is conclusively presumed incapable of forming the requisite intent, while a few other states hold that it is impossible for a child seven or under to commit any tort.

II. Negligence

A. Physical Impairments

77. Physical impairments are taken into account in negligence, and the rule is that a person with a physical impairment must act as a reasonably prudent person with like physical impairment. One court, quoting Dean Prosser, explained:

> As to his physical characteristics, the reasonable man may be said to be identical with the actor. The man who is blind or deaf, or lame, or is otherwise physically disabled, is entitled to live in the world and to have allowance made by others for his disability, and he cannot be required to do the impossible by conforming to physical standards which he cannot meet. Similar allowance has been made for the weaknesses of age and sex. At the same time, the conduct of the handicapped individual must be reasonable in the light of his knowledge of his infirmity, which is treated merely as one of the circumstances under which he acts. A blind man may be negligent in going into a place of known danger, just as one who knows that he is subject to epileptic fits, or is about to fall asleep, may be negligent in driving a car. It is sometimes said that a blind man must use a greater degree of care than one who can see; but it is now generally agreed that as a fixed rule this is inaccurate, and that the correct statement is merely that he must take the precautions, be they more or less, which

102. *Polmatier v. Russ*, 537 A.2d 468 (Conn. 1988).
103. *Bailey v. C.S.*, 12 S.W.3d 159, 162–163 (Tex. App. 2000).

the ordinary reasonable man would take if he were blind. In theory, the standard remains the same, but it is sufficiently flexible to take his physical defects into account.[104]

B. Mental Impairments

78. Negligence does not take into account a person's mental impairment. The Oregon Court of Appeals expressed:

> With respect to liability for negligence, we accept the rule as stated in the Restatement (Second) of Torts s 283B (1965), which provides: "Unless the actor is a child, his insanity or other mental deficiency does not relieve the actor from liability for conduct which does not conform to the standard of a reasonable man under like circumstances'." Among the bases for the rule set forth in comment b to that section are: "1. The difficulty of drawing any satisfactory line between mental deficiency and those variations of temperament, intellect, and emotional balance which cannot, as a practical matter, be taken into account in imposing liability for damage done. 2. The unsatisfactory character of the evidence of mental deficiency in many cases, together with the ease with which it can be feigned, the difficulties which the triers of fact must encounter in determining its existence, nature, degree, and effect; and some fear of introducing into the law of torts the confusion which has surrounded such a defense in the criminal law. Although this factor may be of decreasing importance with the continued development of medical and psychiatric science, it remains at the present time a major obstacle to any allowance for mental deficiency. 3. The feeling that if mental defectives are to live in the world they should pay for the damage they do, and that it is better that their wealth, if any, should be used to compensate innocent victims than that it should remain in their hands. 4. The belief that their liability will mean that those who have charge of them or their estates will be stimulated to look after them, keep them in order, and see that they do not do harm."[105]

C. Children

79. The law of Negligence usually treats children differently from adults. The Illinois Court of Appeals stated:

> If the actor is a child, the standard of conduct to which he must conform to avoid being negligent is that of a reasonable person of like age, intelligence, and experience under like circumstances. Some courts have endeavored to lay

---

104. *Mem'l Hosp. of South Bend, Inc. v. Scott*, 300 N.E.2d 50, 56–57 (Ind. 1973) (citing W. Keeton et al., *Prosser and Keeton on the Law of Torts* 151–152 (4th ed., West Publishing 1971)).

105. *Schumann v. Crofoot*, 602 P.2d 298, 300–401 (Or. Ct. App. 1979) (citing Restatement (Second) of Torts §283B (1965) and cmt. c)).

> down fixed rules as to a minimum age below which the child is incapable of being negligent, and a maximum age above which he is to be treated like an adult. Usually these rules have been derived from the old rules of the criminal law, by which a child under the age of seven was considered incapable of crime, and one over fourteen was considered to be as capable as an adult. The prevailing view is that in tort cases no such arbitrary limits can be fixed. Undoubtedly there is a minimum age, probably somewhere in the vicinity of four years, below which negligence can never be found; but with the great variation in the capacities of children and the situations which may arise, it cannot be fixed definitely for all cases.[106]

Likewise, there is no exact age as to when someone stops being a child, though it is probably somewhere around 13 years of age.

80. One exception to the general rule is when children engage in extremely dangerous activities. The Washington Supreme Court noted:

> Courts in other jurisdictions have created an exception to the special child standard injustice that would occur if a child who caused injury while engaged in certain dangerous activities were permitted to defend himself by saying that other children similarly situated would not have exercised a degree of care higher than his, and he is, therefore, not liable for his tort. Some courts have couched the exception in terms of children engaging in an activity which is normally one for adults only. We believe a better rationale is that when the activity a child engages in is inherently dangerous, as is the operation of powerful mechanized vehicles, the child should be held to an adult standard of care.[107]

For example, a child driving an automobile will be held to the adult standard of care, unless they are so young as to be incapable of committing a tort.

III. Strict Liability

81. Capacity is not considered under strict liability because the focus of strict liability is not on unreasonable conduct or the defendant's intent, but rather on engaging in certain activities recognized by the law as creating strict liability. In the most commonly recognized activity, product liability, it is hard to imagine a child or mentally infirm person being in the chain of culpable sellers. But one can imagine a child or mentally infirm person owning a wild animal—a strict liability activity—and that animal (e.g., a snake or tarantula) injuring another person. Also, a child or mentally infirm person might engage in an abnormally hazardous activity, such as using dynamite they happen to find at a construction site.

---

106. *Appelhans v. McFall*, 757 N.E.2d. 987, 990 (Ill. App. Ct. 2001) (citing Restatement (Second) of Torts §283A and cmt. b (1965)).

107. *Robinson v. Lindsay*, 598 P.2d 392, 393–394 (Wash. 1979).

§5. INTENT

I. General

82. All intentional torts require that the wrongdoer commit a specified act with the requisite intent. The Restatement Second defines intent as "denot[ing] that the actor desires to cause consequences of his act, or that he believes that the consequences are substantially certain to result from it."[108] Intent is therefore met when the actor, subjectively (i.e., in his mind), demonstrates desire or substantial certainty—that fact finder may infer intent from the tortfeasor's actions. A Florida court examining the issue stated:

> The intent with which tort liability is concerned is not necessarily a hostile intent, or a desire to do any harm. Rather it is an intent to bring about a result which will invade the interests of another in a way that the law will not sanction .... To result in liability, the defendant's act must be a voluntary one. But a voluntary act, reduced to its lowest terms, is a contraction of the muscles, and nothing else .... Its legal character must depend upon the actor's surroundings, and his state of mind with respect to them .... Intent, however, is broader than a desire to bring about physical results. It must extend not only to those consequences which are desired, but also to those which the actor believes are substantially certain to follow from what he does .... The practical application of this principle has meant that where a reasonable man in the defendant's position would believe that a particular result was substantially certain to follow, he will be dealt with by the jury, or even by the court, as though he had intended it .... On the other hand, the mere knowledge and appreciation of a risk, short of substantial certainty, is not the equivalent of intent. The defendant who acts in the belief or consciousness that he is causing an appreciable risk of harm to another may be negligent, and if the risk is great his conduct may be characterized as reckless or wanton, but it is not classed as an intentional wrong. In such cases the distinction between intent and negligence obviously is a matter of degree. Apparently the line has been drawn by the courts at the point where the known danger ceases to be only a foreseeable risk which a reasonable man would avoid, and becomes a substantial certainty.[109]

What follows is an explanation, which assumes that culpability moves along a continuum from intent to recklessness, and from recklessness to negligence:

> Intent is not, however, limited to consequences which are desired. If the actor knows that the consequences are certain, or substantially certain, to result from his act, and still goes ahead, he is treated by the law as if he had in fact desired to produce the result. As the probability that the consequences will follow decreases, and becomes less than substantial certainty, the actor's conduct loses

108. Restatement (Second) of Torts §8A (1965).

109. *City of Winter Haven v. Allen*, 541 So.2d 128, 137–138 (Fla. Dist. Ct. App. 1989) (citing W. Keeton et al., *supra* n. 104).

> the character of intent, and becomes mere recklessness .... As the probability decreases further, and amounts only to a risk that the result will follow, it becomes ordinary negligence .... All three have their important place in the law of torts, but the liability attached to them will differ.[110]

II. Substantial Certainty

83. The second way courts establish whether a person had the requisite intent is through the substantial certainty test. One court explained:

> [I]ntentional tortious conduct is when an ordinary, reasonable, prudent person would believe an injury was substantially certain to result from his conduct .... To establish intentional conduct, more than the knowledge and appreciation of risk is necessary; the known danger must cease to become only a foreseeable risk which an ordinary, reasonable, prudent person would avoid (ordinary negligence), and become a substantial certainty.[111]

For example, in one case, a child moved a chair that his aunt was about to sit on, causing great harm to his aunt. The trial court held that the child knew that his aunt was in the process of sitting down and thus was substantially certain she would fall down.[112]

III. Transferred Intent

84. The transferred intent doctrine allows the intent committed in one tresspatory tort to transfer to another tresspatory tort, and also from the intended victim to an unintended victim (i.e., tort to tort, victim to victim, or a combination of both). As one court illustrated the concept:

> If the defendant shoots or strikes at A, intending to wound or kill him, and unforeseeably hits B instead, he is held liable to B for an intentional tort. The intent to commit a battery upon A is pieced together with the resulting injury to B; it is "transferred" from A to B. "The intention follows the bullet ...." His act is characterized as "wrongful," and his fault is regarded as absolute toward all the world, rather than relative to any one person. Having departed from the social standard of conduct, he is liable for the harm which follows from his act, although he did not intend it.[113]

110. Restatement (Second) of Torts §8A, cmt. b. (1965).
111. *Frey v. Kouf*, 484 N.W.2d 864, 867 (S.D. 1992) (citing *VerBouwens v. Hamm Wood Products*, 334 N.W.2d 874, 867, 877 (S.D. 1983)).
112. *Garratt v. Dailey*, 304 P.2d 681 (Wash. 1956).
113. *City of Winter Haven v. Allen*, 541 So.2d 128, 137–138 (Fla. Dist. Ct. App. 1989) (citing W. Keeton et al., *supra* n. 104, at 31–33).

85. This doctrine is however limited to the five tresspatory torts: battery, assault, false imprisonment, trespass to land, and trespass to chattel. At common law, these five torts were all part of the same writ—the writ of trespass—which is why the intent to commit one of them was the intent to commit any of them. The transferred intent doctrine may not be used with other intentional torts, even though another intentional tort may be conceptually related to one of the five tresspatory torts. For example, trespass to chattel and conversion are practically identical, but since conversion originally came from a different common-law writ the transferred intent doctrine does not include conversion.

IV. Mistake

86. Mistake is not a defense to an intentional tort, but in negligence cases, a defendant's mistake is relevant in determining whether there was negligence. If the mistake is one a reasonable person would have made, then it is one factor to consider in assessing whether the particular defendant behaved reasonably under the circumstances.

Chapter 2. Specific Cases of Liability

§1. Liability of Professionals

I. In General: Standard of Care for "Experts"

87. The standard of care expected from professionals is not a higher standard; rather, the standard remains one of reasonableness under the circumstances. However, what is reasonable for a professional is not the same as what is reasonable for a layperson. Rather, a professional is "held to a particularized form of the basic reasonable person standard because in addition to that degree of care, they are expected to possess a higher degree of skill, care, and learning than the average person," at least in the area of his profession.[114] Generally, "[p]rofessionals, … are required not only to exercise reasonable care (i.e., due care) in what they do, but also to possess and exercise a standard minimum of special knowledge and ability" within their specific areas of expertise.[115]

II. Medical Practitioners

88. Medical practitioners can be held liable under two theories of negligence: medical malpractice and informed consent. These two theories are independent of each other even though facts supporting one cause of action may be intertwined with the other. For conduct outside of a physician's professional duties, the normal tort rules apply. For example, a physician that negligently spills some coffee in a hallway in his office, resulting in a patient falling down and being injured, may be liable under the normal negligence rules—the special rules applicable to physicians described in this section would not apply.

A. Medical Malpractice

89. Medical malpractice is a specific category of tort action grounded in negligence principles and its standard rules, as well as being subject to its usual defenses. Medical professionals, however, stand in a special relationship with their patients, based on their status as a professional and a commitment to provide a level of care that is at least comparable to the level of care another professional within that field would also provide. Absent a medical professional undertaking a specific higher level of care with respect to their patient, a professional is expected to treat each patient "with such reasonable diligence, skill, competence, and prudence as are practiced by minimally competent physicians in the same specialty or general field

114. *Advincula v. United Blood Srvcs.*, 678 N.E.2d 1009, 1020 (Ill. 1996).
115. *Ibid.*

of practice throughout the United States."[116] This standard applies not only to medical doctors but also to mental health care providers, dentists, chiropractors, podiatrists, nurses, and other licensed professionals. A court explained medical malpractice as follows:

> To make a prima facie case of medical malpractice, the following elements must be shown: the existence of a duty on the part of the physician to conform to the specific standard of conduct, the applicable standard of care, the failure to perform to that standard, that the breach of duty by the physician was the proximate cause of the plaintiff's injury, and that damages to plaintiff have resulted.[117]

Unlike a general negligence claim, where the reasonable person standard generally remains the same without regard to the specifics of the claim, in a medical malpractice claim the plaintiff must generally use expert testimony to establish the applicable professional standard.[118] This qualifier is not isolated to cases of alleged medical malpractice, with expert testimony usually required to establish any professional standard of care.[119]

90. Not all medical malpractice cases require experts to determine the appropriate standard of care. In some cases, the doctrine of res ipsa loquitur may be used. Under this doctrine, negligence is so obvious that a jury may infer negligence without the aid of an expert. For example, a scalpel or a sponge left in a patient's body would not need an expert to determine the appropriate professional standard of care because under these facts a jury may infer that a surgeon breached his duty of care—it is obvious that scalpels and sponges should not be left in a patient's body.

91. Most importantly, the standard of care is established through custom and not by what a reasonably prudent doctor would do. Thus, breach of duty in a medical malpractice case occurs when a physician fails to follow the custom of the medical profession. If a particular medical custom is used by physicians in the United States then a physician does not commit malpractice if he conforms to custom, even if the particular practice appears unreasonable to a judge or jury—the medical profession is allowed to determine their standard of care.

92. The standard of care for professionals is measured differently from one jurisdiction to another. Historically, courts held a medical professional defendant to the standard of other professionals in the locality in which that medical professional practiced.[120] The modern trend recognizes that all doctors in the United States are trained in the same manner and have similar access to technology and ongoing education. For this reason, modern courts often arrive at the applicable professional

116. *Palmer v. Biloxi Reg'l Med. Ctr.*, 564 So.2d 1346, 1354 (Miss. 1990).
117. *Estate of Northrop v. Hutton*, 9 So.3d 381, 384 (Miss. 2009) (citing *Barner v. Gorman*, 605 So.2d 805, 808–809 (Miss. 1992); *Palmer*, 564 So.2d at 1354–1355).
118. *Palmer*, 564 So.2d at 1355 (quoting *Cole v. Wiggins*, 487 So.2d 203, 206 (Miss. 1986)).
119. *District of Columbia v. Peters*, 527 A.2d 1269, 1273 (D.C. 1987).
120. *See*, e.g., *Small v. Howard*, 128 Mass. 131, 135 (1880).

standard based on state or national customs, although some jurisdictions still follow the traditional locality rule.[121] But even under the national standard, doctors are allowed to practice medicine with the tools available in their community. A doctor in a small rural town, for example, will not be held negligent for failing to order a test that is only available in a few advanced hospitals around the country. Thus, the standard is flexible enough to take into account local conditions.

93. There is not always a single national custom that all doctors must follow—what matters is that a particular custom is followed by a group of doctors in the nation. In one case a surgeon made a wide cut to avoid the nerve to a patient's vocal cords but paralyzed the vocal cords when he cut the nerve. An expert in that case testified that there were surgeons in the United States who would first have located the nerve before making a significant cut, thereby avoiding the possibility of permanently paralyzing the vocal cords. The court held that the surgeon did not commit malpractice because there were other surgeons in the United States who cut wide to avoid paralyzing the vocal cord—this surgeon conformed to a customary medical practice.[122] It is irrelevant that one custom is superior to another custom.

94. All medical professionals are not universally held to the same standard; rather, medical professionals are held to the standard they claim as their own. A medical doctor is held to the standard of a reasonable medical doctor. A chiropractor is held to the standard of a reasonable chiropractor unless said chiropractor claims to have greater skills.[123] A neurosurgeon is held to the standard of an equally specialized neurosurgeon.

B. Informed Consent

95. As mentioned in the general introductory materials to this monograph, American tort law seeks to protect an individual's bodily integrity. Following this principle, tort law in the United States recognizes that patients have the right to determine what is done to their bodies, even if those determinations are contrary to medical recommendations and result in the patient's death. As such, a surgeon who performs a procedure without a patient's consent is liable for battery or negligence absent certain recognized justifications. The informed consent requirement holds that absent a patient's incapacitation, the patient has a right to receive material information pertaining to the nature of any medical procedure a physician is recommending. Material information would include the procedure's risks, its necessity, and any alternative treatments. Materiality is determined using the "patient rule"—what a reasonable patient would view as material. Even when a physician fails to inform a patient of a material risk, a physician will not be held liable if the

121. *See*, e.g., *Bahr v. Harper-Grace Hosps.*, 528 N.W. 170, 172 (Mich. 1995); *Fitzmaurice v. Flynn*, 356 A.2d 887, 891 (Conn. 1975).
122. *Walski v. Tiesenga*, 381 N.E.2d 279 (Ill. 1978).
123. *See Brown v. Shyne*, 151 N.E. 197 (N.Y. 1926).

physician can prove that the patient would have pursued the same course of treatment if he had been informed of the material risk. Also, a patient may not prevail in an informed consent action if the material risk did not actually occur.

96. While the requirement for informed consent seems fairly basic, courts in the United States are divided in their approach to its application. The majority of courts find physicians liable for the intentional tort of battery when they are found to have performed procedures without their patients' informed consent.[124] Virginia is one such jurisdiction, holding that, "[a] surgical operation on the body of a person is a technical battery or trespass unless he or some authorized person consented to it."[125] An increasing minority of jurisdictions, on the other hand, subject physicians to negligence analysis for the same conduct, only holding physicians liable for battery when they perform a surgery that is completely different than the one to which the patient consented.[126]

97. In addition to the duties of physicians in exercising due care in diagnosing and treating their patients, physicians also are responsible for exercising due care when issuing prescriptions. This duty obligates physicians "to inform their patients of those side effects they determine are necessary and relevant for patients to know in making an informed decision," not just in taking medication, but also in the continuance of their daily activities—particularly the use of other medications and the operation of motor vehicles.[127] This duty extends not only to patients but also to any other individuals that patients may foreseeably harm as a result of any inadequate warning, such as other motorists, bicyclists, or pedestrians.[128]

III. Legal Practitioners

98. The various jurisdictions in the United States disagree as to whether legal malpractice is a contract or tort claim, though analytically legal malpractice draws from both areas. The general duty that a legal practitioner owes to his client is the duty "to employ that degree of knowledge, skill, and judgment ordinarily possessed by members of the legal profession" in representing clients.[129] To fulfill this duty, an attorney must act with good faith and in the best interest of his client and must "be familiar with well settled principles of law and the rules of practice which are

124. *Fox v. Smith*, 594 So.2d 596 (Miss. 1992); *Friter v. Iolab Corp.*, 607 A.2d 1111 (Pa. Super. Ct. 1992).
125. *Washburn v. Klara*, 561 S.E.2d 682, 685 (Va. 2002) (citing *Pugsley v. Privette*, 263 S.E.2d 69, 74 (Va. 1980)).
126. *See*, e.g., *Cobbs v. Grant*, 502 P.2d 1 (Cal. 1972); *Kennis v. Mercy Hosp. Med. Ctr.*, 491 N.W.2d 161, 164 (Iowa 1992).
127. *Coombes v. Florio*, 877 N.E.2d 567, 570–571 (Mass. 2007) (citing *Cottam v. CVS Pharmacy*, 764 N.E.2d 814 (Mass. 2002)).
128. *Ibid.*, 571.
129. *Temple Hoyne Buell Found. v. Holland & Hart*, 851 P.2d 192, 198 (Colo. Ct. App. 1992) (citing *Myers v. Beem*, 712 P.2d 1092 (Colo. Ct. App. 1985)).

of frequent application in the ordinary business of the profession."[130] This duty, however, does not include a duty to know every rule; rather, the duty is, as with all negligence actions, a duty to exercise reasonable care in handling the client's matter—a reasonable attorney that is not competent in a particular area of law will either refer a client to another practitioner or become minimally competent in the new area of law. In addition to proving breach of duty, in legal malpractice cases, there must be proof of causation and damages.[131] The following are some particular areas in which legal practitioners may face prosecution for legal malpractice: allowing a statute of limitations to run, failing to prosecute an action, representing clients with conflicting interests, failing to correctly advise a client on the relevant law, failing to prepare or record documents, improperly handling settlement discussions, and using grossly ineffective trial tactics.

99. The courts in some states have found that absent fraud, collusion, or life-endangering negligence, legal practitioners only owe a duty of due care to their clients and to no one else. In other United States jurisdictions, however, in addition to the duty that legal practitioners owe to their clients, attorneys sometimes also have a duty to third-party non-clients. One example of a potential non-client liability is in the case of third-party beneficiaries to wills drafted by attorneys. Because the statute of limitations does not begin to run until the decedent dies, it might be decades before an attorney realizes he committed malpractice decades before. Legal practitioners also generally owe a duty of care to persons seeking their advice (i.e., potential clients) even though those persons may never officially hire the legal practitioner. Finally, there generally is no duty owed to third parties that the attorney knows are in danger because of information the attorney received from a client. Many states allow attorneys to break the attorney-client privilege and warn a third party of possible harm, but only if the harm rises to the level of death or serious bodily harm. But even in those states, there is no requirement that an attorney warns a third party.

IV. Builders and Architects

100. An action for professional negligence may also be maintained for builders, architects, engineers, and surveyors. Such professionals are judged based on a standard of reasonableness as demonstrated against the conduct of members of the same profession exercising "ordinary skill and prudence … under the same or similar circumstances."[132] Unlike many other professional negligence actions, there is no privity requirement for a professional negligence action to proceed against an architect,

130. *Collas v. Garnick*, 624 A.2d 117, 120 (Pa. Super. Ct. 1993).
131. *See*, e.g., *Cummings v. Donovan*, 828 N.Y.S.2d 475, 476 (N.Y. App. Div. 2007) (citing *Simmons v. Edelstein*, 820 N.Y.S.2d 614 (N.Y. App. Div. 2006)).
132. *Bell v. Jones*, 523 A.2d 982, 987 (D.C. 1986).

engineer, builder, or surveyor. Rather, the question of duty in such a case is whether the resultant harm was foreseeable to the particular professional in question.[133]

V. Others

101. Various other professionals may also be subject to professional liability actions. Accountants, for example, have been held liable in some states for professional negligence in failing to exercise reasonable care and competence in the performance of their duties. The applicable standard of care is similar to that of legal and medical professionals: the duty to "render their services with that degree of skill, care, knowledge, and judgment usually possessed and exercised by members of that profession in that particular locality, in accordance with accepted professional standards and in good faith without fraud or collusion."[134] Pharmacists and other drug suppliers may also be held accountable for professional malpractice in negligently dispensing medications, and real and personal property professionals (appraisers, surveyors, brokers, insurance agents, notaries, etc.) may in some states be held accountable for negligence in the performance of their professional duties.

§2. Liability of Public Authorities (Governmental Liability)

I. Federal Government

A. *Overview*

102. The American theory of sovereign immunity developed from the English concept that the king could not be sued in his courts or the courts of his barons. The king was believed to have been divinely appointed and, as such, incapable of wrongdoing; as the monarchy relinquished many of its functions to the state, the state then assumed immunity from suit. Even after America gained its independence from England, the idea of sovereign immunity continued to exist for both federal and state governments. The primary historical exception to this immunity can be found in the Takings Clause of the United States Constitution, which provides that the federal government cannot take private property for public use without paying "just compensation" to the property owner.[135] Although not considered under tort theories of recovery, these constitutionally protected takings are redressible even when the federal government asserts its sovereign immunity.

103. The early rationale for continuing the monarchal notion of governmental immunity in the new republic was primarily to ensure the independence of each governmental branch; specifically, the nation's founders did not want the judiciary

133. *Davidson & Jones, Inc. v. County of New Hanover*, 255 S.E.2d 580, 584 (N.C. Ct. App. 1979), *cert. den'd*, 259 S.E.2d 911 (N.C. 1979).
134. *Rino v. Mead*, 55 P.3d 13, 19 (Wyo. 2002).
135. *See* U.S. Const. Amend. V.

to assert dominion over the legislative and executive branches by hearing suits against them. This fear gave way to practicality as it became accepted that the government, which was set up to ensure and further the welfare of its citizens, should not be accountable for harms in tort—paying out unknown tort claims could have had devastating effects on the government's ability to provide essential services to the entire community. Although some immunity from suit remains at all three levels of government (federal, state, and local), traditional absolute sovereign immunity has been substantially modified or abolished.

B. Federal Tort Claims Act

104. The Federal Tort Claims Act provides a broad waiver of the federal government's sovereign immunity and allows individuals to sue the federal government for torts committed against them. Before suing the federal government in court a plaintiff must submit a claim with the agency responsible for the tort. The federal government has agreed to be sued in federal court using the tort law of the state where the tort occurred. For example, if a tourist is injured while visiting the U.S. Capitol building then the District of Columbia's tort law applies in a civil suit against the federal government.

105. Though the immunity is broad, the federal government retains its immunity for all torts arising out of assault, battery, false imprisonment, malicious prosecution, abuse of process, libel, slander, misrepresentation, and interference with contract. The key to understanding the retained immunity is the "arising under" language of the statute. For example, suppose that a tourist visiting a federal monument is attacked by a criminal. The federal government knew that this particular monument was dangerous to tourists but failed to address the problem. When the tourist brings a negligence action for failing to maintain adequate security, the tort will be reclassified as "arising under" battery and thereby dismissed since the federal government has not waived its immunity for actions arising under battery. The federal government also has not waived its immunity for strict liability torts.

106. The Federal Tort Claims Act also carves out certain activities for which the federal government retains sovereign immunity. Some notable examples include mail delivery, combatant military activities, and all activities that occur outside of the United States. In addition, the federal government retains immunity for all discretionary functions. A discretionary function is one where there is no mandatory statute, policy, or regulation requiring the federal government to act in a certain manner. If the government is not exercising its discretionary function, then it is acting in a ministerial role and must follow the proscribed rules. For example, the federal government may choose to make a military helicopter that does not incorporate safety features into the design. The decision to design that helicopter is within the discretion of the government and the government may not be sued for its negligent design, either directly or indirectly, by suing the independent contractor that made the helicopter for the government.[136]

107. Under all circumstances, an injured person has the right to petition Congress directly with a claim for payment. Prior to the Federal Tort Claims Act, a direct request to Congress was the only way to receive compensation for the federal government's tortious conduct. To receive a payment by Congress, a person needs to find a member of the House of Representatives or the Senate to sponsor a private bill on his behalf. The private bill would need to become law just as any other bill becomes law—it needs to pass both houses of Congress and then be signed by the President. This is an unlikely avenue for tort recovery but one that remains available.

II. State Governments

108. State governments derived their theory of immunity, like the federal government, from the English monarchal system. Since each state is a separate sovereign, each state likewise retains sovereign immunity from most ordinary lawsuits. The founders of the federal government recognized that states might have disputes with one another; therefore, Article III of the United States Constitution provides that states can sue one another before the Supreme Court of the United States.[137] In addition, the Supreme Court imposed eminent domain liability on states identical to that imposed on the federal government by the federal Takings Clause.[138]

109. In addition to the limitations imposed on states' immunity by Congress, most states have enacted their own tort claims acts that, at least to some degree, waive their common-law immunity. Approximately thirty states have abolished their general immunity, retaining it only in limited cases, while others do the opposite and retain their general immunity, waiving it only in specified circumstances. In addition, the legislatures of some states provide that cases against the state are heard by an administrative agency or a specially designated court. Only three states (Alabama, South Dakota, and Wisconsin) retain broad general immunity from suit.

III. Local Governments

110. Unlike state and federal governments, local governments were not established as individual sovereigns and do not enjoy sovereign immunity. But, they do enjoy governmental immunities for a different reason. Historically, the municipality, unlike state and federal government, was not considered a separate entity but

136. *Boyle v. United Technologies Corp.*, 487 U.S. 500 (1988).
137. *See* U.S. Const. Art. III, §2.
138. *Chicago, Burlington & Quincy R.R. Co. v. Chicago*, 166 U.S. 226 (1897).

merely an association of numerous individuals within a locality. Because of this fictional legal status, the municipality could not be sued. Over time, states gradually removed this legal fiction by chartering municipalities and recognizing them as separate legal entities. Long after municipalities were legally recognized as separate entities, states still held them largely immune from suit, generally only assessing tort liability for torts that were committed when the municipality was acting in a proprietary, not governmental, capacity, or in cases of municipality-created nuisance. Gradually, liability was also imposed for negligent maintenance of roads and other negligently maintained municipal property. There is no consensus among the courts as to what test to follow to ascertain whether a municipality is acting in a governmental or proprietary capacity. Some of the various decisions have found that a municipality is acting proprietarily when its activity is done for profit; when it receives a fee for its activity; when the municipality has no duty to its residents to carry out the act; or when the act is one that historically was performed by a private enterprise.[139]

§3. Abuse of Rights (Civil Rights)

111. After the American Civil War, Congress enacted legislation that created what is commonly referred to as a section 1983 claim, allowing people to sue a state or municipal officer for violation of a federal right. The statute reads:

> Every person who, under color of any statute, ordinance, regulation, custom, or usage, of any State or Territory or the District of Columbia, subject, or causes to be subjected, any citizen of the United States or other persons within the jurisdiction thereof to the deprivation of any rights, privileges, or immunities secured by the Constitution and laws, shall be liable to the party injured in an action at law, suit in equity, or other proper proceeding for redress.[140]

A tort claim under section 1983 involves several steps, depending on the particular person or institution to be assessed liability for the civil rights violation. First, in order to "establish liability in an individual capacity claim under §1983, a plaintiff must show that an official, acting under color of state law, deprived the plaintiff of a federal constitutional right."[141] Although supervisory officials are not generally liable for "the unconstitutional acts of their subordinates on the basis of respondeat superior or vicarious liability,"[142] they can be liable under certain circumstances based on one or more of the following factors:

139. *Town of Brunswick v. Hyatt*, 605 A.2d 620 (Md. 1992); *Schulz v. City of Brentwood*, 725 S.W.2d 157 (Mo. Ct. App. 1987); *Blue Fox Bar, Inc. v. City of Yankton*, 424 N.W.2d 915 (S.D. 1988); *Waters v. Biesecker*, 298 S.E.2d 746 (N.C. Ct. App. 1983).
140. Public Health and Welfare Act, 42 U.S.C. §1983 (1979).
141. *Williams v. Barrett*, 287 Fed. Appx. 768, 769 (11th Cir. 2008).
142. *Ibid.* (citing *Cottone v. Jenne*, 326 F.3d 1352, 1360 (11th Cir. 2003); *Hartley v. Parnell*, 193 F.3d 1263, 1269 (11th Cir. 1999)).

> (1) a history of widespread abuse putting the responsible supervisor on notice of the need to correct the alleged deprivation; (2) a supervisor's custodial policy resulting in deliberate indifference to constitutional rights; or (3) facts supporting an inference that the supervisor directed the subordinates to act unlawfully or knew that subordinates would act unlawfully and failed to stop them from doing so.[143]

In addition, the government institution itself may be held liable under section 1983 under the same reasoning as that applying to supervisory officials.[144] The branch of government, whether local or state, however, is important in any section 1983 analysis. The United States Supreme Court has concluded that "*cities, counties, and local officers* sued in their official capacity are themselves 'persons'" under the provisions of section 1983 and, "although they cannot be held vicariously liable … for their subordinate officers' unlawful acts, they may be held directly liable for constitutional violations carried out under their own regulations, policies, customs, or usages by persons having 'final policy-making authority' over the actions at issue."[145] A state official, on the other hand, is not a person under section 1983 and is "immune from liability under the statute by virtue of the Eleventh Amendment and the doctrine of sovereign immunity."[146] But if a state officer enforces an unconstitutional law, he may be sued in his individual capacity.[147]

In many situations, a civil rights violation may be actionable under state law even if it is not actionable under section 1983, as in the case of unconstitutional acts by state officials.[148] One advantage, however, of federal section 1983 claims is that reasonable attorney's fees are available, something generally not available in the United States on the federal level. A full discussion of section 1983 is beyond the scope of this monograph.

§4. Injury to Reputation and Privacy

I. Defamation

A. Overview

112. Although the United States Constitution does not expressly protect an individual's reputation as a fundamental right, the common law highly regards

143. *Williams v. Barrett*, 287 Fed. Appx. at 769 (11th Cir. 2008) (citing *Gonzalez v. Reno*, 325 F.3d 1228, 1234–1235 (11th Cir. 2003)).
144. *See*, e.g., *Arnold v. Metropolitan Government of Nashville and Davidson County*, 2009 WL 2430822, slip op. at 3 (M.D. Tenn. 2009); *Venegas v. County of Los Angeles*, 187 P.3d 1, 4 (Cal. 2004).
145. *Venegas v. County of Los Angeles*, 87 P.3d 1, 4 (Cal. 2004) (citing *McMillian v. Monroe County*, 520 U.S. 781, 784–785 (1997); *Monell v. New York City Dep't of Soc. Srvcs.*, 436 U.S. 658, 690–692 (1978)) (other citations omitted).
146. *Venegas*, 87 P.3d at 5.
147. Ex Parte *Young*, 209 U.S. 123 (1908).
148. *See*, e.g., *Venegas*, 87 P.3d at 13.

reputational integrity, which is what the tort of defamation seeks to protect. The elements of defamation are generally regarded as the following: "(1) the assertion of a false and defamatory statement concerning another; (2) the unprivileged publication of that statement to a third party; and (3) fault amounting at least to negligence by the publisher."[149] In defining a particular statement as defamatory, courts consider "(1) the content, (2) the verifiability, and (3) the context of the challenged statement."[150]

The Supreme Court of the United States altered common-law defamation, creating new rules based on the defamed person's status. The changes began to occur in the 1960s based on the Supreme Court's First Amendment free speech jurisprudence. To avoid confusion, this monograph will first review the common-law rules for defamation, and then discuss how an individual's status alters the rules. As an introductory matter, a private person defamed in a private matter will generally be able to use the common-law rules discussed below.

B. Common-Law Defamation

1. Elements

113. Common-law defamation consists of the following: "(1) a false statement; (2) communicated by speech, conduct or in writing to a person other than the person defamed; and (3) the communication is unprivileged and tends to harm one's reputation so as to lower him or her in the estimation of the community or to deter third persons from associating or dealing with him or her."[151] A person that republishes a defamatory statement is classified as a "repeater" and is liable under defamation, even if the repeater honestly believed the statement was true.

114. A large number of jurisdictions, 24 in 2023, have criminal penalties for defamation. This can create procedural impediments for plaintiffs in civil defamation actions, as defendants can invoke their constitutional right to remain silent to prevent the government from using their testimony in a criminal defamation action. As a matter of practice, governments rarely bring criminal defamation cases.

115. A defamatory statement is one that tends to hold someone up to scorn, ridicule, or contempt, but only when a right-thinking minority of people would find the statement objectionable. For example, a person falsely tells a crowd of people that "Joe is not a murderer," which causes Joe's reputation to be irreparably damaged in the criminal community. That is not actionable under defamation because criminals are not a right-thinking minority. Also, opinions, such as calling someone a "jerk," are not defamatory because opinion statements are neither true nor false and are

149. *Leang v. Jersey City Bd. of Educ.*, 969 A.2d 1097, 1113 (N.J. 2009) (citing *DeAngelis v. Hill*, 847 A.2d 1261 (N.J. 2004)).

150. *Ibid.*

151. *In Re Storms v. Action Wisconsin Inc.*, 750 N.W.2d 739, 748 (Wis. 2008) (citing *Torgerson v. Journal/Sentinel Inc.*, 563 N.W.2d 472 (Wis. 1997)).

understood by others as opinions. In contrast, calling someone a thief is defamatory because it can be proven to be true or false, and it will hurt a person's reputation in the community. Finally, a statement may be defamatory if understood only by a very small segment of society, such as a statement only understood by experts in Babylonian studies.

116. An individual can be defamed if the defamation is directed at a small group. While there is no exact number for group defamation, courts tend to limit defamation to groups that have no more than twenty-five members. In one reported opinion, a person made false and defamatory statements about the salesmen at a department store. Though there were twenty-five salesmen in the store, they were allowed to sue for defamation. *Neiman-Marcus v. Lait*, 13 F.R.D. 311 (S.D.N.Y. 1952). In contrast, someone making a false and defamatory statement about "all law professors in the United States" would not be actionable because that group is too large.

117. A defamatory statement need not be extreme in its presentation to others. Placing a defamatory statement in quotation marks or making a statement in the form of a question will not defeat a defamation action if it is reasonable that others will understand the defamatory nature of the statement. For example, it is defamatory to ask someone in a public meeting: "Is it true or false that you beat your wife?" The implication is that he does in fact beat his wife.

118. The statement must be communicated to someone other than the person being defamed. It can be communicated orally, in writing, or in any other media. The person that makes the statement can be sued if the statement is made in a manner that will reasonably be seen or heard by others. If the person that the statement is directed to self-publishes the statement, then he may not sue for defamation. A person receives a defamatory email, for example, and sends it to others—this is not actionable under defamation because it was self-published.

119. Courts in some jurisdictions recognize compelled self-publication as meeting the publication requirement for defamation. This occurs when someone is improperly terminated from their employment and they are required by a potential new employer to share the false facts from the prior employer's improper termination.

120. Extrinsic facts, those not part of the publication, can be defamatory if those who know the facts can identify the plaintiff. For example, a national publication runs a story about a fictional character, but there are a few dozen people who recognize the character as the plaintiff. In that case, extrinsic facts can be used to allow the plaintiff to sue the publication for defamation.

2. Damages

121. There is a factual distinction drawn between libel and slander. In short, slander is the "oral publication of a false statement," while libel occurs when a false statement is put "in writing or printing."[152] In practice, however, the distinctions between these two causes of action are more substantial. For cases of slander, the slandered party cannot recover from the slanderer unless he can show evidence of actual damages.[153] For libel, damages are presumed and there is no need to show evidence of actual damages.

122. The historical development of the distinctions between spoken and written defamation is pre-colonial and dates back to the fourteenth and fifteenth centuries, where in England, actions of spoken defamation were punished largely through penance instead of monetary damages, whereas actions for written defamation were punished more severely because, especially at that time, "the written or printed word carried great sanction of authenticity" because people believed that the written word was true, and the written word had a much wider circulation than the spoken word.[154] A court reasoned:

> Because of concerns over the printed word and "[t]o prevent dueling and public disorder, where libel was involved, the Star Chamber adopted the rule that if defamation was in print or writing damages would be presumed. It also held that libels of a serious type, since they tended to create duels and breaches of the peace, were crimes. It added that in criminal libel truth was no defense, as it was in civil defamation."[155]

Although the United States has departed from the English common law's somewhat severe historical treatment of libel, it has nonetheless maintained the libel-slander distinction.

123. The common law developed four "slander per se" categories, which if proven allowed for the recovery of presumed damages—common law always presumed damages for libel. The four categories, still maintained by most states, include: statements that question the competence of the defamed person in their employment, accusing someone of having a loathsome disease, accusing someone of a serious crime, and accusing a woman of not being chaste. With this last category, states now apply this category to both men and women. Most states have altered the common law in various ways. For example, some have abolished the slander and libel distinctions and now refer to both as defamation. In these states, slander per se has given way to "defamation per se." Many other states still retain the technical distinction.

152. *Grein v. La Poma*, 340 P.2d 766, 767–768 (Wash. 1959) (citing Spring, *Risks and Rights*, 42, 44, Ch. 4, §§19, 20).
153. *Ibid.*
154. *Ibid.*, 340 P.2d at 768 (citing Spring, *Risks and Rights*, 42, 44, Ch. 4, §§19, 20).
155. *Ibid.*, 340 P.2d at 767–768 (citing Spring, *Risks and Rights*, 42, 44, Ch. 4, §§19, 20).

124. A per se defamatory statement is one in which "the meaning or message is obvious on its face."[156] A per quod defamatory statement is one in which "the defamatory meaning is not clear unless the hearer knows facts or circumstances not contained in the statement itself, and the plaintiff must introduce extrinsic facts to prove the defamatory meaning."[157] A statement itself may be actionable per se, in which instance, "the defendant is presumed to have acted with common-law malice and the plaintiff is presumed to have suffered general damages."[158] Absent a finding that a statement is defamatory per se, the plaintiff bears the burden of proving special damages. Special damages require proving economic loss as a result of the defamation and may include lost business opportunities or termination from employment.

3. Defenses

125. At common law, the plaintiff did not have to prove falsity, and the burden was on the defendant to prove the truth. Today, the burden is on the plaintiff to prove falsity and substantial truth acts as a complete defense to a claim of defamation. Courts employ a "workable test" in assessing whether or not a statement is substantially true so as to defeat a claim of defamation, which is "whether the statement as published would have a different effect on the reader or listener than the truth as pleaded."[159] The reason for this assessment is that "[w]hen the truth is so near to the facts as published that fine and shaded distinctions must be drawn and words pressed out of their ordinary usage to sustain a [defamatory] charge …, no legal harm has been done."[160] For example, a newspaper reports that a person burglarized a house on April 19, 2008, but it was actually burglarized on April 22, 2008. The April 19 date is substantially true.

126. Some privileges are absolute defenses to a defamation claim but are generally limited to certain classes of people. New York courts have explained:

> The absolute privilege "also bars a claim for defamation and is in essence a license to defame for it renders one who defames immune to suit resulting from acts defaming another. The privilege however is reserved for those who are considered principal executives of a state or local government or who are entrusted by law with administrative or executive policy-making responsibilities of considerable dimension."[161]

156. *Erickson v. Jones St. Publishers, L.L.C.*, 629 S.E.2d 653, 664 (S.C. 2006) (citing *Holtzscheiter v. Thomson Newspapers, Inc.*, 506 S.E.2d 497, 501–502 (S.C. 1998)).
157. *Ibid.*
158. *Jones Street Publishers, L.L.C.*, 629 S.E.2d at 664.
159. *Brooks v. Anderson*, 18 Misc.3d 1109(A), 856 N.Y.S.2d 22 (N.Y. Sup. Ct. 2007) (citing *Fleckenstein v. Friedman*, 193 N.E. 537 (N.Y. 1934)) (other citations omitted).
160. *Ibid.*
161. *Ibid.* (citing *Liberman v. Gelstein*, 605 N.E.2d 344 (N.Y. 1992); *Stukuls v. State of New York*, 366 N.E.2d 829 (N.Y. 1977)).

127. Like an absolute privilege, a qualified privilege may also serve as a bar to a defamation claim but is only available in the absence of malice.[162] An example of a qualified privilege is the common interest privilege, which provides that:

> [a] communication made bona fide upon any subject matter in which the party communicating has an interest, or in reference to which he has a duty, is privileged if made to a person having a corresponding interest or duty, although it contained criminating matter which, without this privilege, would be slanderous and actionable; and this though the duty be not a legal one, but only a moral or social duty of imperfect obligation. The rationale underpinning the privilege is that absent abuse, the flow of information between people having a common interest should not be impeded.[163]

When a defendant provides proof of a qualified privilege, the burden shifts to the plaintiff to "come forward with evidence establishing that said statements were motivated solely by express malice or ill."[164] Malice can be proven in one of two ways: common-law malice or actual malice. Common-law malice is defined as "ill will or evil intent as the motive for the defamatory statement and actual malice is statements that were made with a high degree of awareness that said statements were probably false."[165] Actual malice can be proven by "evidence to demonstrate that defendant entertained serious doubts as to the truth of the statement or that he made the same while highly aware that the same was probably false."[166]

128. In addition to the common interest privilege, another common qualified privilege is the public official privilege:

> With regard to said privilege the Supreme Court stated that the profound national commitment to the principle that debate on public issues should be uninhibited, robust, and wide-open, and that it may well include vehement, caustic, and sometimes unpleasantly sharp attacks on government and public officials. Accordingly, a defamatory statement made regarding a public official is immune from liability unless, much like the common interest privilege, plaintiff demonstrates that the same is false and it was made with either actual or common-law malice.[167]

129. A third potential qualified privilege is the limited issue public figure privilege, again reserved for a limited number of people:

> This privilege "is based upon the status of the plaintiff, the burden of proving said status resting on the defendant. A plaintiff is considered a limited issue

162. *Ibid.*
163. *Ibid.*
164. *Ibid.*
165. *Ibid.*
166. *Brooks v. Anderson*, 856 N.Y.S.2d 22 (N.Y. Sup. Ct. 2007) (citing *Liberman v. Gelstein*, 605 N.E.2d 344 (N.Y. 1992); *Stukuls v. State of New York*, 366 N.E.2d 829 (N.Y. 1977)).
167. *Ibid.* (citations omitted).

public figure, and thus a defendant's defamatory statements regarding the same are immune from liability if the plaintiff has voluntarily acted to influence the resolution of a public controversy. In order for the privilege to apply, there must [be] a controversy, and the same must not merely be a matter of public interest, but it must be a real dispute whose outcome affects the general public or some segment in a substantial way. The controversy must be addressing some specific question rather than a general interest or concern. Like the common interest privilege and the public figure privilege, the limited use public figure privilege can be overcome by proof of actual or common law malice."[168]

4. United States Constitutional Constraints

130. Constitutional rulings handed down since the civil rights movement of the 1960s and premised on free speech rights have restructured the American legal system's treatment of common-law defamation. Historically, the United States common law presumed fault, falsity, and damages, but constitutional decisions have overturned all three presumptions, depending on the status of the defamed person. Beginning in 1964, the Supreme Court started recognizing that the federal constitution's First Amendment's free speech provisions impose certain limitations on assessing strict liability in defamation cases. Currently, the constitutional rules that are applicable to defamation cases are as follows:

1. In *New York Times Co. v. Sullivan*, 376 U.S. 254 (1964), if the plaintiff is a public official, a candidate for public office, or a public figure, the plaintiff must prove the elements of defamation under state tort law and that the defendant published (1) a false statement; (2) knowing the statement to be false or acting in reckless disregard of the statement's truth or falsity. The plaintiff must prove these constitutionally mandated elements with convincing clarity.[169]
2. In *Gertz v. Robert Welch, Inc.*, 418 U.S. 323 (1974), if the plaintiff is a private person but the issue involved in the publication is one of public concern, the plaintiff must prove the elements of defamation under state tort law and also that the defendant (1) published a falsehood; (2) that, at a minimum, he was negligent or otherwise at fault in failing to ascertain or state the truth; and (3) that the plaintiff suffered actual injury (i.e., special damages) to reputation as a result.[170]
3. In *Dun & Bradstreet, Inc. v. Greenmoss Builders, Inc.*, 472 U.S. 749 (1985), if the plaintiff is a private person and the alleged defamation is of no public concern, the plaintiff does not have to prove actual damages but can recover

168. *Ibid.*
169. *New York Times Co. v. Sullivan*, 376 U.S. 254 (1964).
170. *Gertz v. Robert Welch, Inc.*, 418 U.S. 323 (1974).

presumed damages. In addition, in such cases, all of the common-law presumptions remain viable to the plaintiff.[171]

II. Invasion of Privacy

A. *Overview*

131. Tort law in the United States recognizes four separate privacy interests, from which four separate torts have risen to provide an individual with relief if these interests are interfered with. These torts are:

1. intrusion into seclusion;
2. appropriation of name or likeness;
3. false light; and
4. public disclosure of private facts.[172]

Intrusion into seclusion and appropriation of name or likeness enjoy the most acceptance, while the other two are accepted by a minority of the states.

B. *Intrusion into Seclusion*

132. Tort liability for intrusion into seclusion or solitude is generally defined by the Second Restatement of Torts as follows: "One who intentionally intrudes, physically or otherwise, upon the solitude or seclusion of another or his private affairs or concerns, is subject to liability to the other for invasion of his privacy, if the intrusion would be highly offensive to a reasonable person."[173] A plaintiff in this action must also show that the interference with his seclusion is substantial, "of a kind that would be highly offensive to the ordinary reasonable man, as the result of conduct to which the reasonable man would strongly object."[174] A reporter, for example, wants to interview a new mother concerning the birth of her couplets. The mother refuses, but the reporter continues to call at all hours of the day and night and sends daily emails requesting an interview. The reporter is liable for intruding into her seclusion.

C. *Appropriation of Name or Likeness, and the Right of Publicity*

133. The elements of the common-law privacy tort of appropriation of name or picture are as follows: "(1) the defendant's use of the plaintiff's identity; (2) the

171. *Dun & Bradstreet, Inc. v. Greenmoss Builders, Inc.*, 472 U.S. 749 (1985).
172. *See* W. Prosser, *Privacy*, Calif. L. Rev. 48, 383 (1960).
173. *Castro v. NYT Television*, 895 A.2d 1173, 1177 (N.J. Super. App. Div. 2006) (citing Restatement (Second) of Torts §652B (1977)).
174. *Ibid.*

appropriation of plaintiff's name or likeness to defendant's advantage, commercially or otherwise; (3) lack of consent; and (4) resulting injury."[175] Establishing all of these elements, however, still does not automatically "provide relief for every publication of a person's name or likeness."[176] Rather, First Amendment freedom of speech and freedom of the press rights must be balanced against the right of privacy that this tort seeks to protect.[177]

Many states have codified this tort, providing protection of a person's name or likeness after death because at common law this tort action ended at the plaintiff's death. Statutes generally allow the heirs or assign a period of time to protect the decedent's name or likeness. For example, the State of California allows a decedent's name or likeness to be protected for seventy years after the decedent's death.[178] But a person or heir must bring a claim within the statute of limitations, which usually begins to run at the time of publication.

The amount of damages can also be extremely high. In one case a model was paid USD 250 to pose for two hours for a coffee advertisement that was to be used in Canada. A few years later the coffee company started using the photos in the United States without consulting or paying the model. When the model contacted the coffee company, eleven years after the photographs were taken, they stopped using the photo and paid another model USD 10,000 for using his photograph for the next ten years. The model sued the coffee company for using his likeness without permission, and a jury awarded him USD 15 million in damages—10% of the coffee company's profits because the jury believed his picture was responsible for the successful coffee sales.[179]

D. False Light

134. False light is a privacy tort "involving publicity that unreasonably places [the plaintiff] ... in a false light before the public."[180] A person faces tort liability for false light when he:

> gives publicity to a matter concerning another that places the other before the public in a false light [and] (a) the false light in which the other was placed would be highly offensive to a reasonable person, and (b) the actor had knowledge of or acted in reckless disregard as to the falsity of the publicized matter and the false light in which the other would be placed.[181]

175. *Gionfriddo v. Major League Baseball*, 114 Cal.Rptr.2d 307, 313–314 (Cal. Dist. Ct. App. 2001) (citations omitted).
176. *Ibid.*
177. *Ibid.*
178. California Civil Code §3344.1 (2008).
179. *Christoff v. Nestle USA, Inc.*, 213 P.3d 132 (Cal. 2009) (in which the California Supreme Court remanded the case for a determination as to whether the single publication rule applied).
180. *Romaine v. Kallinger*, 537 A.2d 284, 293–294 (N.J. 1988) (citing Restatement (Second) of Torts §652E (1977)).
181. *Ibid.*

Like defamation, false light requires publication and falsity, "or else at least have the capacity to give rise to a false public impression as to the plaintiff."[182]

Unlike defamation, false light actions do not require proof that the "material that casts plaintiff in a false light also injure her standing in the community."[183] The false material must, however, "constitute a major misrepresentation of [plaintiff's] character, history, activities or beliefs ... [and must be] of a character highly offensive to a reasonable person."[184] Because false light is so similar to defamation, some courts have refused to recognize the tort and instead instruct litigants to sue under defamation. For example, Frank became a hero after he saved the lives of many people by foiling a terrorist attack. A motion picture studio created a film depicting Frank's bravery but added a fictitious romance with a woman he met during the foiled attack. Frank was married at the time of his bravery to another woman and the studio knew the romance was false, but Frank was not defamed by the movie. The motion studio company is liable for placing Frank in a false light.

E. Public Disclosure of Private Facts

135. Public disclosure of private facts is the least recognized privacy tort. Its elements are as follows: "(1) publicity was given to the disclosure of private facts; (2) the facts were private, and not public, facts; and (3) the matter made public was such as to be highly offensive to a reasonable person."[185] Usually, in order to meet the publicity component of this tort, "a plaintiff must show that the information was disclosed to the public at large; however, the publicity requirement may be satisfied where a disclosure is made to a small number of people who have a 'special relationship' with the plaintiff."[186] There is some question as to whether this tort is compatible with contemporary free speech protections.

§5. Interference with Contractual Relations

136. To prove the tort of interference with contractual relations, the plaintiff must prove the following:

1. a valid contract between the plaintiff and a third party (i.e., someone other than the defendant);
2. defendant's knowledge of the contract;
3. defendant's intentional act that induced the breach of contract;
4. actual breach of contract; and
5. actual provable damage.

---

182. *Ibid.*
183. *Ibid.*
184. *Ibid.*
185. *Cordts v. Chicago Tribune Co.*, 860 N.E.2d 444, 450 (Ill. App. Ct. 2006) (citing *Miller v. Motorola Inc.*, 560 N.E.2d 900, 902–903 (Ill. App. Ct. 1990)).
186. *Ibid.*

For a full discussion, *see* Chapter 3, §3 below.

§6. Battery

137. A battery occurs when a person intentionally causes a harmful or offensive touching of another. One divisive issue involves the intent that is necessary to commit a battery: some courts require the intent to contact and the intent to harm or offend (i.e., dual intent), while others only require the intent to contact (i.e., single intent). Those that have adopted the single intent rule require a wrongdoer to desire or know to a substantial certainty that contact will occur, resulting in a harmful or offensive touching. The states that have adopted the dual intent requirement require the same intent to contact as above, but they also require an intent to harm or offend. The "actor [has] to understand that his contact [will] be harmful or offensive."[187] Some of the confusion arises from the Restatement (Second) of Torts, which states:

> According to the Restatement (Second) of Torts, (1) An actor is subject to liability to another for battery if (a) he acts intending to cause a harmful or offensive contact with the person of the other or a third person, or an imminent apprehension of such a contact, and (b) an offensive [or harmful] contact with the person of the other directly or indirectly results. (2) An act which is not done with the intention stated in Subsection (1, a) does not make the actor liable to the other for a mere offensive contact with the other's person although the act involves an unreasonable risk of inflicting it and, therefore, would be negligent or reckless if the risk threatened bodily harm.[188]

138. The fact finder determines what is harmful or offensive under the circumstances, both of which operate on a continuum. A harmful contact is easier to prove and includes gunshots, punches to the face, or a kick to the shin. What constitutes offensive contact can be more difficult to prove. The general rule is that a contact must be offensive to a reasonable person; thus, normal touchings allowed by society are usually not offensive. For example, a person approaches an acquaintance and taps them on the shoulder. This is a normal behavior in society and would not be an offensive touching. However, if a person touches another with the knowledge that the other person does not want to be touched, then the touching is offensive because a reasonable person aware of the victim's desire would not have touched him. "Contact with the body is offensive if it offends a reasonable sense of personal dignity."[189] Also, "causing an offensive touching, even indirectly to another's clothing and not resulting in injury, is the tort of battery."[190] In one case the plaintiff was waiting in a buffet line when a club employee took the plate out of the plaintiff's

187. *White v. Muniz*, 999 P.2d 814, 816–817 (Colo. 2000).

188. *Ibid.*, 816 (citing Restatement (Second) of Torts §18 (1965)).

189. *Cooper v. Albacore Holdings*, 204 S.W.3d 238, 246 (Mo. Ct. App. 2006) (quoting *J.D. v. M.F.*, 758 S.W.2d 177, 178 (Mo. Ct. App. 1988)).

190. *Selmeczki v. N.M. Dept. of Corr.*, 129 P.3d 158, 167 (N.M. Ct. App. 2006) (citing *State v. Ortega*, 827 P.2d 152, 155–156 (N.M. Ct. App. 1992)).

hands and told him he could not eat in the club. The court found that this constituted a battery, even though the plaintiff was not touched by the defendant.[191]

139. Once a battery occurs the victim may recover all reasonable damages, even when the wrongdoer did not and could not have foreseen the severity of the damages. For example, a person lightly kicks another person, hoping to cause no harm at all. But the kicking victim suffers from hemophilia—a condition that prevents the blood from clotting—and incurs thousands of dollars in damage. The wrongdoer is liable for all damages, including any emotional harm suffered by the plaintiff.

§7. Assault

140. The tort of assault occurs when a defendant intentionally acts to cause a victim reasonable apprehension of an imminent harmful or offensive contact. Under criminal law, civil assault would be labeled as an "attempted battery." Assault is ancient, entering Anglo-American jurisprudence in 1348. It is often referred to as a tort that protects a touching of the mind and not touching of the body. Among non-lawyers, there is confusion between criminal assault and civil assault because the word assault is used colloquially to describe a physical attack. Criminal assault is closest to the tort of battery and not to the tort of assault, and the crime of attempted assault is closest to the tort of assault because civil assault does not have a touching component. If physical contact occurs, the proper tort is a battery.

141. "An act is done with the intent of putting the other in apprehension of an immediate harmful or offensive contact if it is done for the purpose of causing such an apprehension or with knowledge that, to a substantial certainty, such apprehension will result."[192] For example, a person that takes a ball and throws it at a point a few millimeters near the victim's head is liable for assault because they knew that the victim would be apprehensive of an imminent contact. But if the intended victim is blind or does not notice the ball approaching them, there is no assault as one must perceive that contact is about to occur. In other words, the victim must be aware of the assault at the time it occurred.

142. The majority of states follow the traditional rule and require that the apprehension be reasonable, while a minority of states follow the Restatement (Second) of Torts approach and allow any apprehension, reasonable and unreasonable, to be actionable. One important issue is whether words, by themselves, can create an assault. The following is one court's explanation:

> An assault is "an act intended to put another person in reasonable apprehension of an immediate battery, and which succeeds in causing an apprehension

191. *Fisher v. Carrousel Motor Hotel, Inc.*, 424 S.W.2d 627 (Tex. 1967).
192. *Jordan v. Wilson*, 5 So.3d 442, 448 (Miss. Ct. App. 2008), *cert. den'd*, 11 So.3d 1250 (Miss. 2009) (citing Restatement (Second) of Torts §21, cmt. d (1965)).

> of such battery. Words in themselves, no matter how threatening, do not constitute an assault; the actor must be in a position to carry out the threat immediately, and he must take some affirmative action to do so."[193]

But "[w]ords are never spoken in a vacuum, and they cannot be utterly divorced from past conduct, or from the accompanying circumstances"[194] and "may be highly relevant under the tort law definition of assault to determining whether the fear or apprehension in the victim was reasonable."[195] Though some courts refer to fear, all that is needed is reasonable apprehension. Assume, for example, that a very old man with a knife threatens a highly trained soldier. While the soldier may never experience fear, he may be apprehensive about getting cut.

143. Finally, the tort requires immediacy. A significant delay between the act that causes apprehension and the time when the threatened contact occurs can defeat the claim. For example, a person tells the victim that he is going to beat him up in a week. The victim may be apprehensive, but the beating is not imminent. Even thirty minutes might not be sufficiently imminent.

§8. False Imprisonment

I. Overview

144. The tort of false imprisonment seeks to redress interference with one's general freedom and personal liberty. "Although nuances vary from state to state, the gist of the common-law tort is conduct by the actor which is intended to, and does, in fact, confine another within boundaries fixed by the actor where, in addition, the victim is either conscious of the confinement or is harmed by it."[196] Improper motive or hostility by the defendant toward the plaintiff is not a required component of the intent element of this tort; the intent to confine is sufficient. The confinement also does not have to be for any minimum period of time to be tortious; rather, "[t]he restraint requirement of this action requires … simply sufficient time for one to recognize his illegal restraint … [and] is complete with even a brief restraint of the plaintiff's freedom."[197] An honest or reasonable mistake is not a valid defense.[198]

---

193. *Krochalis v. Insurance Co. of North America*, 629 F.Supp. 1360, 1370 (E.D. Pa. 1985) (citing *Cucinotti v. Ortmann*, 159 A.2d 216 (Pa. 1960)).
194. *Clark v. Virginia*, 676 S.E.2d 332, 336 (Va. Ct. App. 2009) (quoting Restatement (Second) of Torts §31 cmt. d (1965)).
195. *Ibid.*, at 337.
196. *McCann v. Wal-Mart Stores, Inc.*, 210 F.3d 51, 53 (1st Cir. 2000) (citing Restatement (Second) of Torts §35 (1965)).
197. *West v. King's Dept. Store, Inc.*, 365 S.E.2d 621, 624 (N.C. 1988) (citing 68 W. Keeton et al., *supra* n. 70, at §11).
198. *McCann v. Wal-Mart Stores, Inc.*, 210 F.3d 51, 53 (1st Cir. 2000).

II. Bounded Area

145. The defendant must be in an area with fixed boundaries imposed by the defendant.[199] These boundaries need not be as concrete as the four walls of a room and may be satisfied by merely restraining the plaintiff's movement. Even large areas, like a city or state, may qualify as a bounded area.[200] But one court held that the bounded area prong was not met by a plaintiff falsely imprisoned in Taiwan because, even though he could not leave the country, he was still free to move throughout the entire nation of Taiwan.[201] In other words, his liberty interest was not sufficiently impaired to justify compensatory damages.

146. If the plaintiff has a reasonable means of exit, however, he has not been confined at all. Specifically, "[t]he confinement within the boundaries fixed by the defendant must be complete; if there is a known, safe means of escape, involving only a slight inconvenience, there is no false imprisonment."[202] However, a person that uses heroic efforts to escape may still claim that he was falsely imprisoned. For example, a victim whose only exit is a window and ledge on a ten-story building will prevail in a false imprisonment action even if he quickly escapes through the window and enters an unlocked room on the other side of the building.

III. Means of Confinement or Restraint

147. The clearest way to show confinement is by establishing the use of a physical barrier or restraint, such as locking someone in a building or pinning someone against a wall.[203] But a person can also be physically confined by blocking a vehicle, taking someone's keys, or detaining other personal property that would prevent someone from leaving a specific area because it is not reasonable for a person to leave their personal property against their will.[204]

148. Confinement can also be shown through other less stringent means. "It is generally settled that mere threats of physical force can suffice, and it is also settled … that the threats may be implicit as well as explicit, and that confinement can also be based on a false assertion of legal authority to confine."[205] For verbal threats

199. *See*, e.g., *Faniel v. Chesapeake and Potomac Tel. Co. of Maryland*, 404 A.2d 147, 150 (D.C. 1979).
200. *Albright v. Oliver*, 975 F.2d 343 (7th Cir. 1992).
201. *Shen v. Daly*, 222 F.3d 472 (8th Cir. 2000).
202. *Chicarelli v. Plymouth Garden Apartments*, 551 F.Supp. 532, 541 (E.D. Pa.1982).
203. *Geddes v. Daughters of Charity of St. Vincent De Paul, Inc.*, 348 F.2d 144, 147 (5th Cir. 1965); *Stockett v. Tolin*, 791 F.Supp. 1536, 1556 (S.D. Fla. 1992).
204. *Ibid.* (citing *Schanafelt v. Seaboard Fin. Co.*, 239 P.2d 42 (Cal. Ct. App. 1951); *Verstraelen v. Kellog*, 372 P.2d 543 (Wash. 1962); *Burrow v. K-Mart Corp.*, 304 S.E.2d 460 (Ga. Ct. App. 1983)).
205. *McCann v. Wal-Mart Stores, Inc.*, 210 F.3d 51, 53 (1st Cir. 2000).

to constitute confinement, they "must be sufficient for a person to be placed in reasonable apprehension of force."[206] Such reasonable apprehension of force is not present when, for example, a person is confronted with an alarm, the threat of job loss, or other moral pressures.[207]

IV. Improper Assertion of Legal Authority (False Arrest)

149. False arrest is a subset of the tort of false imprisonment when unlawful confinement is committed by law-enforcement officers or others who assert the authority to arrest. To prove false arrest, "a plaintiff must establish that the defendants were without legal authority to arrest and detain him and that the detention was not accomplished pursuant to accepted legal procedures."[208] Law-enforcement officers are not liable for false arrest if they are privileged to have confined the plaintiff, as in the following two examples: "(1) an arrest pursuant to a warrant; or (2) an arrest without a warrant in which the officer has 'probable cause', that is, reasonable objective grounds to believe that a crime was committed and that the plaintiff committed it."[209] Shopkeepers may detain suspected shoplifters, but in many states, they do so at their own peril—if they detain a person that did not actually steal any goods then the shopkeeper may be sued for false imprisonment. The shopkeeper's good faith or reasonable belief is irrelevant. A number of states have enacted laws that allow shopkeepers to detain a suspected shoplifter if they have reasonable suspicion that their goods were stolen.

150. The tort of false arrest does not require the initiation of formal proceedings, whereas the torts of malicious prosecution and abuse of process do. To succeed on a claim for malicious prosecution, a plaintiff must prove that the defendant "(1) … initiated a prior criminal proceeding against him, (2) … did not have probable cause to initiate such a proceeding, (3) the proceeding was instituted maliciously, and (4) it terminated in [the plaintiff's] favor."[210] To succeed on a claim for abuse of process, a plaintiff must show that a legal proceeding, "although set in motion in proper form, [became] perverted to accomplish an ulterior or a wrongful purpose for which it was not designed."[211] In addition, the common-law tort of malicious prosecution, unlike false arrest, requires proof of actual malice.[212] For a full discussion of these other torts, *see* paragraph 193 below.

---

206. *Zavala v. Wal-Mart Stores, Inc.*, 393 F.Supp.2d 295, 334 (D.N.J. 2005).
207. *Ibid.*
208. *Krantz v. City of Toledo Police Dep't*, 365 F.Supp.2d 832 (N.D. Ohio 2005) (citing *McFinley v. Bethesda Oak Hosp.*, 607 N.E.2d 936 (Ohio Ct. App. 1992)).
209. *Dunn v. Felty*, 226 S.W.3d 68, 71 (Ky. 2007) (citing D.B. Dobbs, *The Law of Torts* §36, 67–69 (West Group 2000)).
210. *Beaudoin v. Levesque*, 697 A.2d 1065, 1067 (R.I. 1997) (citing *Solitro v. Moffatt*, 523 A.2d 858, 861–862 (R.I.1987)).
211. *Ibid.*
212. *See*, e.g., *Dyson v. City of Pawtucket*, 670 A.2d 233, 239 (R.I. 1996).

V. Consciousness of Confinement

151. The tort of false imprisonment requires that the detained person either be aware of the detention or harmed by the detention. Originally, under the position taken by the First Restatement (and followed by most jurisdictions), a person could not incur liability for false imprisonment unless the victim was aware of his confinement. After criticism of this position, the Second Restatement moved away from this position and expanded liability for false imprisonment to cases in which "the person physically restrained knows of the confinement *or is harmed by it*."[213] In support of this modification of the prior awareness requirement, the Second Restatement stated:

> An example of injury resulting from false imprisonment, where the victim is not even aware of the confinement, appears in the Restatement. "A, a diabetic, is suffering from shock brought on by an overdose of insulin. B believes A to be drunk, and without any legal authority to do so arrests A and locks him up over night in jail. In the morning A is released while still unconscious and unaware that he has been confined. On learning what has occurred A is greatly humiliated, and suffers emotional distress, with resulting serious illness. B is subject to liability to A for false imprisonment." Thus, a victim may be entirely unaware of confinement and still suffer harm as a result of the false imprisonment, as in the Restatement's example of the diabetic. Or, a victim may perceive the confinement, as in our example of the prisoner unknowingly incarcerated beyond his release date, yet not be contemporaneously aware the confinement was unlawful. In either situation, the false imprisonment results in harm.[214]

VI. No Minimum Time

152. There is no minimum time requirement for the tort of false imprisonment. Rather, "[t]he offense of false imprisonment occurs when a defendant acts 'to confine one intentionally without lawful privilege and against his consent within a limited area for any appreciable time, however short.'"[215] Even a relatively short confinement can result in a large compensatory damages award because a person's liberty interest is highly valued.

---

213. *Scofield v. Critical Air Med., Inc.*, 45 Cal. App. 4th 990, 1003–1006 (Cal. App. 2 Dist 1996) (citing Restatement (Second) of Torts §42 (1934); W.L. Prosser, *False Imprisonment: Consciousness of Confinement*, 55 Col. L. Rev. 847).

214. *Ibid.*

215. *Fryerson v. Ohio Dept. of Rehab. & Corr.*, 778 N.E.2d 153, 155 (Ohio Ct. Cl. 2002) (citing 1 Fowler V. Harper & Fleming James, *The Law of Torts* 226, sec. 3.7 (1956); *Feliciano v. Kreiger*, 362 N.E.2d 646 (Ohio 1977)).

VII. Transferred Intent

153. The principle of transferred intent also applies to the tort of false imprisonment. Intent can transfer between any one of the five tresspatory torts: battery, assault, trespass to chattels, trespass to land, and false imprisonment. Also, intent to imprison one person can transfer to a stranger. "Under this doctrine the intention to confine any person is a sufficient intent to render one liable to the person actually confined. It is immaterial that the actor did not know the identity of the person he intended to confine; nor does it matter that the actor intended to affect some person other than the one actually confined."[216]

§9. Interference with Property Interests

I. Real Property

A. *Trespass to Realty*

154. Trespass to real property occurs when a person enters the land of another without the owner's consent.[217] The only intent required for trespass is "that of the actor to enter the property" of another, and an honest or reasonable mistake as to the land's actual owner does not negate the requisite intent for the tort of trespass.[218] Trespass can occur in numerous situations of interference with real property. "The intrusion can occur when an actor intentionally enters land possessed by someone else, or when an actor causes something else to enter the land."[219] Trespasses of the latter sort often occur when actors place objects on or under the property of another, either without the owner's knowledge or consent, or leave objects on the property past the limits of the initial permission from the owner.

What constitutes real property *v.* personal property can vary from state to state. Generally, the land and anything permanently affixed to land will qualify as real property. While there are no difficulties in defining land, there can be some difficulties in determining if a particular piece of property is permanently affixed to the land or not. For example, a restaurant may have a large neon sign inside the restaurant. If the sign is secured by a few nails to a wall and could be removed, there could be an issue of whether it is permanently affixed to the wall or not.

B. *Waste*

155. Waste allows a property owner to recover damages from a prior property owner who was in lawful possession of the land when the damages occurred. There

216. *Adams v. National Bank of Detroit*, 508 N.W.2d 464, 468 (Mich. 1993) (citing *Du Lac v. Perma Trans Prods., Inc.,* 163 Cal. Rptr. 335 (Cal. Dist. Ct. App. 1980)).
217. *Wilen v. Falkenstein*, 191 S.W.3d 791, 797 (Tex. App. 2006).
218. *Ibid.*, 798.
219. *Hoery v. U.S.*, 64 P.3d 214, 217–218 (Colo. 2003) (citations omitted).

are three elements to this tort. First, there must be an act to the reality that is deemed to be waste, which includes misuse, destruction, alteration, or neglect. Second, the act must have been done by someone who was in legal possession of the reality. And third, the act must prejudice the interest of another. Waste occurs in several contexts, including landlord-tenant, joint tenancy, and mortgagor-mortgagee.[220] In addition to physically damaging the property, waste includes failing to keep mortgage covenants (e.g., maintaining adequate insurance), and failing to pay property taxes. States have various versions of this tort, including California, which adds bad faith to the elements of the tort.[221]

II. Personal Property

A. *Trespass to Chattels*

156. The tort of trespass to chattels requires proof that a defendant "had either actual or constructive possession" of the personal property of another "and that there was an unauthorized, unlawful interference or dispossession of the property."[222] Americans highly value property ownership rights, including the right to exclude others from using their property. Therefore a property owner does not need to prove actual harm to recover at least nominal damages for the tort of trespass to chattel.[223] A plaintiff may recover the amount to repair or replace the chattel, depending on the severity of the trespass.

B. *Conversion*

157. The tort of conversion is very similar to trespass to chattels, with the plaintiff needing to prove:

> (1) he has a right to the property; (2) he has an absolute and unconditional right to the immediate possession of the property; (3) he made a demand for possession; and (4) the defendant wrongfully and without authorization assumed control, dominion, or ownership over the property.[224]

Property can include conversion of money so long as it can be described as a specific chattel, and conversion may include documents containing intangible rights. In cases involving documents containing intangible rights, "the damages include the value of such rights. However, intangible property rights cannot be the subject of

220. *Mannick v. Wakeland*, 117 P.3d 919 (N.M.App., 2004).
221. *Cornelison v. Kornbluth*, 15 Cal. 3d 590 (1975).
222. *Kirschbaum v. McLaurin Parking Co.*, 656 S.E.2d 683, 686 (N.C. Ct. App. 2008) (citations omitted).
223. *Ibid.*
224. *The Film and Tape Works, Inc. v. Junetwenty Films, Inc.*, 856 N.E.2d 612, 623–624 (Ill. App. Ct. 2006) (citations omitted).

conversion unless they are merged into a tangible document over which the alleged tortfeasor exercised dominion or ownership."[225]

158. There are two important differences between trespass to chattels and conversion. The first is historical and often not significant. Trespass to chattels is one of the five tresspatory torts between which transferred intent operates. If a person wants to use the transferred intent doctrine, then he must plead trespass to chattels and not conversion. Second, the damages between the torts can be different. Establishing conversion requires the defendant to pay the fair market value of the property that was taken—it operates as a forced sale of the property. Establishing trespass to chattels may result in an award for the full fair market value of the damaged property or it might result in a lesser amount. Thus, the person suing for conversion must prove that a forced sale of the property is the only just result, and if that is not proven, then the case will be lost. For example, a person driving a brand-new car might be upset when someone scratches the car's paint. But if they sue for conversion because they want another new car they will lose the lawsuit.

C. Power to Transfer Goods[226]

159. A person that purchases personal property receives the title that the transferor had the power to transfer. So if a purchaser buys stolen property, even in good faith, he does not receive good title to the property and can be sued by the true owner for trespass to chattel or conversion. For the vast majority of personal property, title is a legal fiction, in the sense that there are no government agencies that track personal property ownership. Automobiles and airplanes are two notable exceptions where the government tracks property ownership through formal title registration procedures. There are a few instances where a good faith purchaser does receive good title. First, when the original owner is deceived as to the true identity of the transferor. Second, the exchange between the original owner and the transferor was by check and the check was later dishonored. Third, the original owner and transferor agreed to a cash sale. Fourth, the delivery to the transferor was accomplished through fraud deemed illegal by criminal law. And fifth, sales by a merchant that sells the types of goods in question (e.g., a watch merchant illegally sells a watch that the true owner had left with it for repair).

§10. Negligence

I. Overview

160. Negligence is the most important tort and is used in many civil actions in many different situations. To prove negligence, a claimant "must prove … the following elements: '(1) a duty of care owed by the defendant to the plaintiff; (2)

225. *Ibid.*
226. Uniform Commercial Code §2-403.

conduct by the defendant falling below the standard of care amounting to a breach of that duty; (3) an injury or loss; (4) cause-in-fact; and (5) proximate or legal cause.'"[227] While the cause of action is called negligence, some courts refer to duty and breach of duty as negligence, thereby causing some confusion.

II. Duty and the Standard of Care

161. Only those that owe a duty to another can be sued under negligence. Generally, this means that a person must act, but in some cases failing to act might implicate the duty owed to another. The question of whether someone owes a duty to another is a question of law; therefore, a judge can dismiss a case when no duty is owed. There has been some debate as to how often a judge should exercise this dismissal authority, especially in cases when there arguably is a question as to whether the defendant owed the plaintiff any duty.

In one of the most celebrated cases of the early twentieth century, *Palsgraf v. Long Island Railroad*, two men were running to catch a moving train. When a conductor tried to help one of the men get on the train he dislodged a package in that passenger's hands. Unknown to the conductor the small package contained fireworks, which caused an explosion and injured the plaintiff, Mrs. Helen Palsgraf. New York's highest court held that Mrs. Palsgraf was an unforeseeable plaintiff and thus ruled that the railroad did not owe her a duty of care, even though the jury had awarded her damages.[228] Concerned with overly sympathetic juries many courts in the first half of the twentieth century analyzed unforeseeable plaintiffs under the duty element, thereby keeping cases from the jury. Today, most courts analyze foreseeability under proximate cause, thereby allowing the jury to decide on any disputed questions. But, courts are free to exercise their discretion and determine duty questions, though today they are likely to exercise that discretion only when it is obvious that a defendant did not owe any duty to the plaintiff.

When a duty exists then the next issue is determining the appropriate standard of care. The standard of care can be determined by a civil statute (rare), negligence per se, the person's status in relation to someone or something, or the default reasonably prudent person standard.

162. The reasonable person is a legal fiction created by the courts to be used as a standard by which an actor's conduct is gauged in cases of claimed negligence. This standard of reasonableness generically describes the duty that all people owe to one another—to exercise ordinary care in their activities so as to minimize or avoid harming each other. Courts invariably apply this default standard in negligence cases unless the defendant has assumed a higher standard of care or a different standard has been imposed by statute.

227. *Downs ex rel Downs v. Bush*, 263 S.W.3d 812, 818 (Tenn. 2008) (citing *West v. East Tenn. Pioneer Oil Co.*, 172 S.W.3d 545, 550 (Tenn. 2005)).
228. *Palsgraf v. Long Island Railroad Co.*, 162 N.E. 99 (N.Y. 1928), *reh'g denied*, 164 N.E. 564 (N.Y. 1928).

163. The Restatement of Torts offers a definition of the reasonable person in the comments to section 283 as a person who exhibits the characteristics of ordinary "attention, knowledge, intelligence and judgment."[229]As such, the reasonable person standard is objective in that it is based on certain traits assumed to be possessed by all members of society. This standard, however, is also subjective in the sense that it also takes into account the actual circumstances faced by a particular defendant at the time of his act or omission in determining whether his conduct is unreasonably risky and thus negligent.[230]

A. *Emergency*

164. Although often referred to as the emergency doctrine, the issue of emergency is not really a doctrine at all but is merely a factor in determining the reasonableness of an actor's behavior. The emergency doctrine can arise in numerous contexts, though it most often arises in motor vehicle collisions. The emergency doctrine contemplates that an actor may be confronted with an unforeseeable and sudden emergency and may have a limited amount of time within which to act. Harm caused in such a scenario does not necessarily mean that an actor behaved unreasonably and the emergency must be taken into account in gauging his conduct. However, a danger that is foreseeable and can be prepared for is by definition not a sudden emergency and is not covered by this doctrine.

165. In *Regenstreif v. Phelps*, the Kentucky Supreme Court succinctly described the sudden emergency doctrine:

> The sudden emergency doctrine does not excuse fault; it defines the conduct to be expected of a prudent person in an emergency situation .... "[W]hen a defendant is confronted with a condition he has had no reason to anticipate and has not brought on by his own fault, but which alters the duties he would otherwise have been bound to observe, then the effect of that circumstance upon these duties must be covered by the instructions." In Kentucky, sudden emergency qualifications have been approved in automobile collision cases in which the defendant driver has encountered a patch of ice on the roadway or children or animals darting into the roadway. Kentucky also recognizes that other situations such as other vehicles, swooping airplanes or falling boulders, could conceivably create an emergency for a driver that would justify a sudden emergency qualification. In explaining why the qualification needs to be given in cases where a driver encounters an ice patch, our predecessor court stated: "While the driver must take into consideration the slippery condition of the highway, ... if the evidence shows that the accident resulted from a condition of the road and not from any negligence of the driver, no liability results, since

229. Restatement (First) of Torts §283 cmt. a (1934).
230. *Ibid.*, cmt. b.

it is common knowledge that an automobile may skid on a slippery highway without any negligence on the part of the operator."[231]

B. Physical Conditions

166. Negligence is based on the legal fiction created by the reasonable person standard, against which an individual's behavior is measured. Over time, this standard has become recognized as being flexible with regard to the elderly or those with physical disabilities. Specifically, the "law does not demand that the blind shall see, or the deaf shall hear, or that the aged shall maintain the traffic agility of the young."[232] The Second Restatement of Torts describes the reasonable person standard with regard to persons having physical disabilities as follows:

> If the actor is ill or otherwise physically disabled, the standard of conduct to which he must conform to avoid being negligent is that of a reasonable man under like disability. Thus the standard of conduct for a blind man becomes that of a reasonable man who is blind. This is not a different standard from that of the reasonable man but an application of it to the special circumstances of the case.[233]

For more information, *see* paragraph 77 above.

C. Mental Conditions

167. Although tort law applies the reasonable person standard differently to persons with physical disabilities, it makes no allowances for persons with mental deficiencies. "[I]n a negligence action a mentally ill or insane person is held to the same standard of care as an ordinarily careful person under the circumstances."[234] Many policy reasons support this determination:

> including the difficulty of distinguishing true incapacity from mere bad judgment, the belief that the custodians of incompetents will be encouraged by the rule to watch them more closely and keep them under control, and the perceived sense of fairness, even in the absence of moral blame, of a rule requiring mental defectives who live among the rest of society to conform to the general standards of conduct or pay their innocent victims for the damage they cause.[235]

231. *Reenstreif v. Phelps*, 142 S.W.3d 1, 4–5 (Ky. 2004) (citing *Harris v. Thompson*, 497 S.W.2d 422 (Ky. 1973)) (additional citations omitted).
232. *Bernard v. Russell*, 164 A.2d 577, 578 (N.H. 1960).
233. *Ibid.* (Citing Restatement (Second) of Torts §283(c), cmt. a (1965)).
234. *Galindo v. TMT Transport, Inc.*, 733 P.2d 631, 632 (Ariz. Ct. App. 1986).
235. *Ibid.*, (citing W. Keeton et al., *supra* n. 104, at §32, 177–178 (footnotes omitted)).

For more information, *see* paragraph 78 above.

D. *Effect of Superior Abilities, Skill, or Knowledge*

168. Although tort law makes no allowances for persons with substandard mental capacity, it does take into account increased knowledge in particular cases, as in physicians and other persons of special knowledge and skills. As explained by one court:

> [I]f a person in fact has knowledge, skill, or even intelligence superior to that of the ordinary person, the law will demand of that person conduct consistent with it. Experienced milk haulers, hockey coaches, expert skiers, construction inspectors, and doctors must all use care which is reasonable in light of their superior learning and experience, and any special skills, knowledge or training they may personally have over and above what is normally possessed by persons in the field.[236]

E. *Effect of Minority*

169. A minor is generally held to the standard of a reasonable child "of like age, intelligence, and experience under similar circumstances."[237] An exception to this general rule is when a child engaged in an activity that "is normally undertaken only by adults, and for which adult qualifications are required [or] … a professional activity which requires special skill … ."[238] In such a case, when a child engages in an adult activity, he will be held to the adult standard of care.[239] For more information, *see* paragraph 79 above.

III. Unreasonableness (Breach of Duty)

A. *Overview*

170. Once it is determined that a person owes a duty to another and the standard of care is established, the next issue is whether that standard of care was breached. When negligence per se or a civil tort statute establishes the standard of care then breach occurs when the statute is violated. *See* Chapter 1, §3, II above. But most tort actions use the default standard of care—the reasonably prudent person—and

236. *Jackson v. Axelrad*, 221 S.W.3d 650, 655–656 (Tex. 2007) (citing Restatement (First) of Torts §289 (1934); Restatement (Second) of Torts §289 (1965); W. Keeton, et al., *Prosser and Keeton on Torts* §32, 185).

237. *Thomas v. Inman*, 578 P.2d 399, 403 (Or. 1978) (citing Restatement (Second) of Torts §283A (1965); *Simmons v. Holm* et al., 367 P.2d 368 (Or. 1961)).

238. *Inman*, 578 P.2d at 403; *Simmons*, 367 P.2d 368.

239. *Ibid.*

breach is established when someone exposes another at an unreasonable risk of harm. The jury alone is charged with determining whether the conduct was unreasonable under the circumstances.

One way of establishing unreasonableness is deviation from custom. The plaintiff may introduce evidence of some custom and the jury may consider it during their deliberations. But juries are not required to find breach of duty based on deviation—the deviation from custom is merely evidence for them to consider. For example:

> Carl is a guest at the Finney Hotel. The bathroom in the hotel includes a shower, protected by a sliding door made of ordinary glass. Carl trips while taking a shower and falls on the door. Its glass shatters and lacerates Carl. It is a standard practice among hotels to use shatter-proof tempered safety glass rather than ordinary glass at hazardous locations, such as shower enclosures. Finney's departure from this custom is some evidence of its negligence.[240]

Just as deviating from custom is not conclusively a breach of duty, following custom does not conclusively establish reasonable conduct. The jury may decide that a custom is unreasonable and that a defendant was negligent for following the custom.

When courts examine breach of duty, on appeal or at summary judgment, courts usually use some version of a risk-utility formula. The courts compare the utility of the conduct and the burden of avoiding harm against the likelihood of harm and the seriousness of harm. While courts use this approach on appeal, juries are not generally told that they are to use a risk-utility formula in making their decision.

B. *Res Ipsa Loquitur*

171. In some cases there is no direct evidence establishing the defendant's negligence and the only evidence is circumstantial. In those cases, a plaintiff may request the use of res ipsa loquitur, which means "the thing speaks for itself." In the first case discussing the concept a barrel of flour fell out of a second-story window, injuring a person walking on the street. The court noted that barrels do not fall out of windows absent someone's negligence.[241] The rule is explained as follows:

> Res ipsa loquitur applies where a plaintiff demonstrates the following elements: "1) the instrumentality causing the damage must be under the exclusive control of the defendant, 2) the occurrence must be such as in the ordinary course of things would not happen if those in control of the instrumentality used proper care, and 3) the occurrence must not be due to any voluntary act on the part of the plaintiff. Where the elements of res ipsa loquitur are met, a rebuttable presumption of negligence is raised. Additionally, the requirement of exclusive control of the damaging instrumentality does not limit res ipsa

240. Restatement (Third) of Torts: Liab. Physical Harm §13 (2005) (Illust. 2).
241. *Byrne v. Boadle Court of Exchequer*, 2 H. & C. 722, 159 Eng. Rep. 299 (1863).

loquitur to a single defendant; the doctrine may be applicable where authority is shared concerning the instrumentality in question."[242]

Another res ipsa loquitur formulation is that the injury probably occurred because of negligence and the defendant is probably responsible for the negligence. Circumstantial evidence, by its very nature, involves probability and res ipsa loquitur is a doctrine that attempts to limit circumstantial evidence to situations that have a higher probability of being true. If the jury accepts the circumstantial evidence then they may infer that the defendant acted unreasonably.

IV. Injury or Harm

172. Part of the plaintiff's prima facie case is establishing harm. If harm is not proven then the negligence action will fail. Harm can include damage to property or person, and may include stand-alone emotional harm. Unlike intentional torts, nominal damages are generally not available. Proving actual harm becomes important in cases where the defendant's conduct rises to a level where punitive damages can be awarded, but if there is no actual harm then the case must be dismissed for failing to establish a prima facie case.

§11. Emotional Harm

I. Intentional Infliction of Emotional Distress

173. Tort law recognizes the importance of one's emotional wellbeing and, as such, imposes liability on those who cause certain legally recognized emotional harms. Intentional infliction of emotional distress is one of the causes of action that allows for stand-alone emotional harm recovery. A majority of jurisdictions define the tort of intentional infliction of emotional distress with the following four elements:

1. extreme and outrageous conduct;
2. intent or reckless disregard;
3. a causal connection between the conduct and injury; and
4. severe emotional distress.

A plaintiff can satisfy the intent requirement with evidence of the defendant's "desire or purpose to accomplish the harm, or by evidence that such harm was substantially certain to occur."[243] Transferred intent, however, does not apply, since intentional infliction of emotional distress is not one of the five tresspatory torts, and

242. *Thomas v. Bradley*, 978 So.2d 1020, 1026 (Miss. Ct. App. 2008) (citing *Coleman v. Rice*, 706 So.2d 696, 698 (Miss. 1997); *Read v. S. Pine Elect. Power Ass'n*, 515 So.2d 916, 919–920 (Miss. 1987)).

243. *Kjerstad v. Ravellette Publ'ns, Inc.*, 517 N.W.2d 419, 429 (S.D. 1994); *Jackson v. Sun Oil Co. of Pennsylvania*, 521 A.2d 469, 471 (Pa. Super. Ct. 1987).

in any event, this tort requires the specific intent to cause severe emotional harm, or in the alternative to act with reckless disregard of the plaintiff's rights.[244]

174. Although many forms of conduct may cause emotional distress, the only conduct that is actionable as the tort of intentional infliction of emotional distress is conduct that "recitation of the facts to an average member of community would arouse his resentment against the actor, and lead him to exclaim, 'Outrageous!'"[245]

Many courts look to the Second Restatement for guidance on the definition of outrageous conduct, and in their analyses courts generally agree that extreme and outrageous conduct is not proven just because a:

> defendant has acted with an intent which is tortious or even criminal, or that he has intended to inflict emotional distress, or even that his conduct has been characterized by malice, or a degree of aggravation which would entitle the plaintiff to punitive damages for another tort. Liability has been found only where the conduct has been so outrageous in character, and so extreme in degree, as to go beyond all possible bounds of decency, and to be regarded as atrocious, and utterly intolerable in a civilized community.[246]

175. Determining what conduct is outrageous is dependent upon the prevailing cultural values and norms of society, as well as certain factors that may be unique to the individuals in a particular case. Proving outrageousness of the defendant's conduct is not an easy task. Four general predictors (i.e., "markers of outrage") have arisen that generally support a finding of outrage on the part of the defendant, specifically when he inflicts emotional harm through any of the following:

1. by abusing a position of power;
2. by taking advantage of a plaintiff whom the defendant knows to be particularly vulnerable;
3. by continuing certain acts which in isolation may be merely offensive, at times when the plaintiff is unable to leave in order to avoid such offensive acts; or
4. by physically harming or threatening to physically harm a person or property of special interest to the plaintiff.[247]

In each of these circumstances the defendant manipulates a disparity in power between himself and the plaintiff to inflict emotional harm, thus seriously offending society and rendering the conduct outrageous for tort purposes.

In some cases what might not be extreme or outrageous to the vast majority of society might be so to a particular individual when the person committing the act is aware of the plaintiff's vulnerability. In one case a plaintiff believed that a pot of gold was hidden on the land of a distant relative after learning its location from a

---

244. *See*, e.g., *Christensen v. Superior Court*, 820 P.2d 181, 203–204 (Cal. 1991).
245. *Mellaly v. Eastman Kodak Co.*, 597 A.2d 846, 848 (Conn. Super. Ct. 1991) (quoting Restatement (Second) of Torts §46 cmt. d (1965)).
246. *McMahon v. Craig*, 97 Cal. Rptr.3d 555, 566 (Cal. Dist. App. Ct. 2009) (citations omitted).
247. *See* Restatement (Second) of Torts §46 (1965) and comments.

fortune teller. The landowner, a distant cousin, gave her permission to dig on his property. After several months the distant cousin decided to play a practical joke on the plaintiff and to that end hid an old pot with some rocks in the area in which she was digging. When she found the pot she took it to a local bank and found a judge to open it with her. When she opened it was devastated and suffered severe emotional harm because she believed she had found the buried treasure. The court explained that the distant cousin knew the plaintiff had been in mental institutions and that because he knew of her mental infirmity his actions were culpable under intentional infliction of emotional distress.[248]

176. The intent requirement for the tort of intentional infliction of emotional distress is met when the actor directly intends that the plaintiff be subjected to severe emotional distress or in cases in which "the act is done ... with knowledge on the part of the actor that severe emotional distress is substantially certain to be produced by his conduct."[249] No personal hostility between the defendant and the plaintiff is required to satisfy this element.[250]

177. The mental distress suffered by plaintiff due to defendant's outrageous conduct must be intolerable based on an objective standard (i.e., no reasonable person could have been expected to have endured defendant's conduct). The severity of the distress must be proven and must also be causally linked to the defendant's outrageous conduct. Although expert testimony is the primary means of proving the severity of a plaintiff's emotional distress, expert testimony witness evidence is not required, and the issues of causation and severity are generally issues to be determined by the fact finder.[251]

178. A minority of states require that severe emotional harm be established by the plaintiff exhibiting physical manifestations of the emotional harm.[252] In those jurisdictions, courts look favorably on conditions such as bleeding ulcers or speech disorders, while conditions like insomnia or nervousness are disfavored because they are emotional rather than physical. All courts in the United States require some evidence to prove severe emotional distress; sometimes, the outrageousness of the defendant's conduct is sufficient evidence without additional proof, and sometimes it is not. In any event, merely being upset about a person's conduct is never sufficient to prove severe emotional distress.[253]

---

248. *Nickerson v. Hodges*, 84 So. 37 (La. 1920).
249. *Leaf River Forest Prods., Inc. v. Ferguson*, 662 So.2d 648, 666 (Miss. 1995) (citing *Lyons v. Zale Jewelry Co.*, 150 So.2d 154, 158 (Miss, 1963)); *see Public Finance Corp. v. Davis*, 360 N.E.2d 765, 771–772 (Ill. 1976) (citing Restatement (Second) of Torts §46 (1965)).
250. *Leaf River Forest Prods., Inc.*, 662 So.2d at 666.
251. *Mellaly v. Eastman Kodak Co.*, 597 A.2d 846, 847 (Conn. Super. Ct. 1991) (quoting Restatement (Second) of Torts §46 cmts. h & j (1965)).
252. *See*, e.g., *Bendross v. Town of Huntersville*, 582 S.E.2d 726 (N.C. Ct. App. 2003), in which the North Carolina courts limit severe emotional distress to "any emotional or mental disorder, such as, for example, neurosis, psychosis, chronic depression, phobia, or any other type of severe and disabling emotional or mental condition which may be generally recognized and diagnosed by professionals trained to do so."
253. *See*, e.g., *Hatch v. State Farm Fire and Cas. Co.*, 930 P.2d 382 (Wyo. 1997).

179. Third parties are allowed to recover for intentional infliction of emotional distress in certain circumstances, even if the conduct at issue was not directed at them. Generally, for a third party to recover, he must be a witness to the act and must also be "a close relative of the person against whom the outrage is directed."[254] In addition, recoveries are usually allowed, not just when the conduct was outrageous, but when the conduct was also "unquestionably violent and shocking."[255] In circumstances in which the defendant knows that a third party is present while he is acting outrageously toward another person and they are likely to suffer emotional harm, then, under a theory of substantial certainty, it necessarily follows that the defendant also intends that the third party suffer emotional harm.

II. Negligent Infliction of Emotional Distress

180. In the past, the common law did not generally provide recovery for someone who suffered stand-alone emotional distress because of the negligent act of another. In almost every case emotional harm could be claimed only when it was parasitic to a tort where there was physical injury or another underlying tort such as defamation. The one notable exception involved the situation where a defendant negligently handled the dead body of a close relative—in that rare circumstance a plaintiff could historically recover for their stand-alone emotional harm.

181. Modern courts generally allow recovery for "stand-alone emotional harms" caused by negligence, provided that the emotional harm was foreseeable and causally connected to the negligent act. In addition, courts generally require that a plaintiff recover only when a reasonable person would have suffered severe emotional distress and the plaintiff in fact suffered that level of distress (objective and subjective standard). Despite these general requirements, there is otherwise little consensus among the states as to the essential elements for the tort of negligent infliction of emotional distress. A slim majority of states only allow those plaintiffs that can establish physical manifestations of their emotional harm to recover. For example, a bleeding ulcer would be a physical manifestation while insomnia would generally not qualify as a physical manifestation.

182. Three primary reasons exist for this lack of uniformity among the states regarding negligent infliction of emotional distress:

1. the problem of permitting legal redress for harm that is often temporary and relatively trivial;
2. the danger that claims of mental harm will be falsified or imagined; and

---

254. *Nelson v. City of Las Vegas*, 665 P.2d 1141, 1145 (Nev. 1983) (citing William Prosser, *Handbook of the Law of Torts* §12, 62 (4th ed., West Publishing 1971)).
255. *Ibid.*

3. the perceived unfairness of imposing heavy and disproportionate financial burdens upon a defendant, whose conduct was only negligent, for a consequence which appears remote from the "wrongful" act.[256]

Because of these problems, courts take differing approaches to these claims:

> The most frequently adopted principles include: (1) denying recovery for emotional injuries without accompanying bodily harm or other compensable damage to the plaintiff, (2) denying recovery unless the plaintiff is in the "zone of danger," (3) denying recovery unless the plaintiff has "sensory observation" of the event causing the third party's injuries, (4) requiring the existence of a special relationship between the plaintiff and the injured party, and (5) denying recovery unless the injury to the other person is, or is reasonably perceived to be, serious.[257]

183. Although largely abandoned by modern courts, a minority of jurisdictions still follow the impact rule for negligent infliction of emotional distress claims and require physical contact in order to permit recovery for negligently inflicted emotional harm. For example, Florida still follows the impact rule and will not permit recovery for negligently inflicted emotional harm "unless some physical injury had been inflicted and the mental injury was so connected that is was not severable from the physical injury."[258] Jurisdictions that follow this traditional rule, however, have created exceptions to it and have also gradually broadened their definitions of impact to allow recovery. Florida courts, again, have stated that "[t]he essence of impact, then, it seems, is that the outside force or substance, no matter how large or small, visible or invisible, and no matter that the effects are not immediately deleterious, touch or enter into the plaintiff's body."[259]

184. The zone of danger rule is followed by a majority of jurisdictions, has been abandoned by some jurisdictions, and largely expanded by others in modern American tort law. An extension itself from the impact rule, the zone of danger rule provides that, even if a person is not physically impacted by a tortfeasor's negligent act, they may still recover for negligently inflicted emotional distress provided that, at the time of the act, "(1) he was within the 'zone of danger' of an act negligently directed at him by defendant; (2) he was subjected to a reasonable fear of immediate personal injury; and (3) he in fact suffered substantial bodily injury or illness as a result."[260] In effect, the zone of danger rule is a means to focus attention on the proximate cause element of negligence. Normally, a defendant is the proximate cause of an injury if the harm is reasonably foreseeable. Under negligent infliction of emotional distress, only certain types of foreseeable injuries qualify for

256. *Eskin v. Bartee*, 262 S.W.3d 727, 733–734 (Tenn. 2008) (citing W.P. Keeton, *Prosser and Keeton on the Law of Torts* §54, 360–361 (West Publishing 1984)). (other citations omitted).
257. *Ibid.*
258. *Futch v. Wal-Mart Stores, Inc.*, 988 So.2d 687, 691 (Fla. Dist. Ct. App. 2008).
259. *Eagle-Picher Indus., Inc. v. Cox*, 481 So.2d 517, 527 (Fla. Dist. Ct. App. 1985).
260. *Brueckner v. Norwich University*, 730 A.2d 1086, 1092 (Vt. 1999).

recovery—specifically, only those that can be tied to being in the zone of danger. The zone of danger is the area where a person is at risk of physical harm.

185. Courts in the United States generally require a present injury to allow recovery. "[A] present fear as to a future harm is not a compensable element of damages if there is no reasonable basis established for the fear being entertained and no increased possibility of the consequence feared developing as a result of the injuries sustained."[261] Conversely, the reverse scenario is implied in this rule that is, "that if there is a reasonable basis for the fear of future harm and the possibility of that harm developing was increased as a result of the negligently caused injury, the mental distress is compensable."[262] As noted by one court:

> [C]ommentators have argued that courts should limit recovery for emotional distress, including fear, because of "(1) the problem of permitting legal redress for harm that is often temporary and relatively trivial; (2) the danger that claims of mental harm will be falsified or imagined; and (3) the perceived unfairness of imposing heavy and disproportionate financial burdens upon a defendant, whose conduct was only negligent, for consequences which appear remote from the 'wrongful' act" … These concerns should lead courts in such cases to restrict recovery to compensation for severe emotional distress arising from serious fear occasioned by a substantial, medically verifiable, possibility of contracting the disease … A small probability of contracting disease must be balanced against the probable harm if the disease is contracted to determine whether a plaintiff has alleged adequate grounds for recovering for severe emotional distress … [E]ven a foreseeable fear of deadly disease may not be compensable if the feared contingency is too unlikely.[263]

186. Third-party recovery is allowed when the third party was also in the zone of danger. Some courts also require that the person primarily injured by the tortfeasor have been a close relative of the witnessing party.[264] The resulting bodily injury or illness "is due to the unique experience of having witnessed, at such close range as to be in the 'zone of danger', the event that caused the injury to the other person … ."[265] Courts that have adopted this rule will not allow recovery absent some physical manifestation of emotional distress (i.e., injury). The rationale for this requirement comes from the Restatement Second of Torts, which provides that requiring physical manifestations of emotional disturbances as a prerequisite to recovery for negligent infliction of emotional distress is justified by three reasons:

---

261. *Brantner v. Jenson*, 352 N.W.2d 671, 672 (Wis. Ct. App. 1984) (citing *Howard v. Mt. Sinai Hospital, Inc.*, 217 N.W.2d 383, 388 (Wis. 1974)).
262. *Ibid.*
263. *Majca v. Beekil*, 682 N.E.2d 253, 255 (Ill. App. Ct. 1997) (quoting W. Keeton et al., *supra* n. 70, at §54, 360–361) (other citations omitted).
264. *See*, e.g., *Keck v. Jackson*, 593 P.2d 668, 670 (Ariz. 1979) (citing W. Prosser, *The Law of Torts* §54, 334–335 (4th ed., 1971)).
265. *State Farm Mut. Auto. Ins. Co. v. Dowdy*, 192 P.3d 994 (Alaska 2008).

> One is that emotional disturbance which is not so severe and serious as to have physical consequences is normally in the realm of the trivial, and so falls within the maxim that the law does not concern itself with trifles. It is likely to be so temporary, so evanescent, and so relatively harmless and unimportant, that the task of compensating for it would unduly burden the courts and the defendants. The second is that in the absence of the guarantee of genuineness provided by resulting bodily harm, such emotional disturbance may be too easily feigned, depending, as it must, very largely upon the subjective testimony of the plaintiff; and that to allow recovery for it might open too wide a door for false claimants who have suffered no real harm at all. The third is that where the defendant has been merely negligent, without any element of intent to do harm, his fault is not so great that he should be required to make good a purely mental disturbance.[266]

187. The modern trend is away from requiring third parties to be in the zone of danger. For example, should a mother that is not in the zone of danger be able to recover from seeing her only daughter get run over by a negligently driven automobile? A large number of states would allow recovery under these facts, but they also use the proximate cause element as a way of limiting who may recover. These states tend to allow foreseeable plaintiffs to recover, which generally means only close relatives who either witnessed the harm or arrived shortly after the injury. As with any stand-alone emotional harm tort, the harm must be severe.

§12. Pre-natal Harm

I. Overview

188. Historically, no tort liability existed toward a fetus prior to its birth because there was no recognized duty owed to an unborn child.[267] This no-duty concept has been rejected by modern courts, which impose tort liability for harm sustained by a fetus provided that certain requirements are met: first, that the child was born alive or if born dead, was viable at the time of the injury. Recovery would be dependent on the wording of a state's wrongful death statute.

II. Wrongful Conception

189. Wrongful conception, a type of medical malpractice, is brought for an unwanted pregnancy that resulted due to a failed sterilization procedure, abortion, or contraception. It is not necessary that the resulting child be impaired in any way; rather, the gist of the tort lies in the birth being unwanted or unexpected by the parents, regardless of whether the child is born perfectly healthy. The jurisdictions that

---

266. *Ware ex rel. Ware v. ANW Special Educ. Co-op. No. 603*, 180 P.3d 610, 618 (Kan. Ct. App. 2008) (quoting Restatement (Second) of Torts §436A cmt. b (1965)) (other citations omitted).
267. Restatement (Second) of Torts §869(1) cmt. a (1979).

recognize wrongful conception as tortious generally do not allow recovery for child-rearing expenses. Rather, these jurisdictions usually limit damages "to the hospital and medical expenses of the pregnancy, the cost of sterilization, pain and suffering connected with the pregnancy, and loss of the mother's wages during that time."[268]

III. Wrongful Birth

190. Unlike wrongful conception actions, which do not require any harm to be sustained by the child, a wrongful birth action involves a child born with one or more defects that could have been detected by a physician. When the physician committed medical malpractice by not finding the defect or failing to inform the mother of the defects, the physician took away from the mother the option of aborting the baby. Even a mother that would not have aborted her baby can likely recover since the alleged harm is the lost choice. A wrongful birth claim must meet all the elements of general negligence claims (duty, breach, causation, and damages).[269] In addition, a plaintiff in a wrongful birth action must show the existence of "an undisclosed fetal risk [which] was material to a woman in her position; the risk materialized, was reasonably foreseeable and not remote in relation to the doctor's negligence; and, had plaintiff known of that risk, she would have terminated her pregnancy."[270] For this reason, a wrongful birth claim is a form of informed consent action that seeks to protect a potential mother's freedom of choice in deciding whether to continue a particular pregnancy. Damages include all costs related to the birth and child-rearing costs at least until the age of majority. There is some debate as to whether all child-rearing costs are available or only the difference between rearing a healthy child and a disabled child.

§13. Third-Party Claims: Loss of Consortium

191. A tortfeasor is liable not only to the person that was injured but also to the spouse of that person. The nature of the claim arises from the tangible and intangible harm suffered by the spouse, including the loss of household services, companionship, solace, comfort, affection, and sexual services. For example, driver negligently injures husband in an automobile accident and husband can no longer engage in sexual activities. Wife may recover from driver under a loss of consortium claim for her loss. Though this claim derives from the underlying tort, it is an independent claim that can be brought by the injured spouse. This is true even when the tortfeasor settles the claim against the spouse he injured initially. In the situation where the only lawsuit involves a loss of consortium claim, the plaintiff must first establish the underlying tort to prevail on the loss of consortium claim.

---

268. *Kingsbury v. Smith*, 442 A.2d 1003, 1006 (N.H. 1982).
269. *See*, e.g., *Coleman v. Dogra*, 812 N.E.2d 332, 337 (Ohio Ct. App. 2004).
270. *Canesi ex rel. Canesi v. Wilson*, 730 A.2d 805, 824 (N.J. 1999).

192. In recent years, courts have been asked to expand loss of consortium to include significant others, cohabitants, fiancées, parents, and children. Courts have been reluctant to expand the tort, fearing multiple recoveries or fraudulent claims, while some courts have avoided the issue by noting that the modern basis for the tort is loss of sexual services.

§14. TORTIOUS LITIGATION

193. Those that improperly use the criminal or civil court system may be held civilly liable. Malicious prosecution is potentially available for successful defendants in a criminal proceeding, and in civil litigation, a successful defendant may recover for malicious institution of civil proceedings. Because of the general rule that litigants in the United States must pay for their own litigation (i.e., the "American Rule"), courts are hesitant to award attorney fees to successful defendants—in England, the "British Rule" is followed, which requires the losing party to pay for the attorney fees of the winner. Because it is unusual to award attorney fees in the United States, these torts are reserved for defendants that not only win their lawsuits but can also prove some wrongful act in commencing the litigation or wrongful act during the litigation.

I. Malicious Prosecution and Malicious Institution of Civil Proceedings

194. To succeed on a claim for malicious prosecution a plaintiff must prove that the defendant "(1) … initiated a prior criminal proceeding against him, (2) … did not have probable cause to initiate such a proceeding, (3) the proceeding was instituted maliciously, and (4) it terminated in [the plaintiff's] favor."[271] Malice in this context does not mean evil intent, but rather a wrongful or ulterior purpose. Many older cases placed the burden of proving good faith on the defendant, but most jurisdictions today have shifted the burden of proving malice to the plaintiff.

II. Abuse of Process

195. Abuse of process claims deals with improper actions taken during legitimate litigation. To succeed on a claim for abuse of process a plaintiff must show that a legal proceeding, "although set in motion in proper form, [became] perverted to accomplish an ulterior or a wrongful purpose for which it was not designed."[272] For example, an accountant rents a small office and discovers in winter that the heat does not work. Accountant decides to withhold a small amount of rent for what he

---

271. *Beaudoin v. Levesque*, 697 A.2d 1065, 1067 (R.I. 1997) (citing *Solitro v. Moffatt*, 523 A.2d 858, 861–862 (R.I.1987)).

272. *Ibid.*, 1068 (citing *Hillside Associates v. Stravato*, 642 A.2d 664, 667 (R.I.1994)).

believes is the diminished value of the office. Landlord sues accountant for withholding rent, which landlord knows accountant cannot legally do. To harass accountant, landlord fails to show up at court on three different occasions, though each time accountant showed up after closing his office for the day. In an abuse of process claim, accountant should be successful for landlord's actions and collect for his lost income on the days he closed his office.

§15. Alienation of Affections

196. Seven states still recognize the tort of alienation of affections. This tort protects both spouses from interference in the marital relationship, with most cases focusing on sexual misconduct with someone outside the marriage. The elements of this tort include: (1) a marriage with love and affection existing between husband and wife; (2) that love and affection were alienated; and, (3) the malicious acts of the defendant produced the loss of that love and affection. By "love and affection" courts do not mean that the marriage relationship must be wonderful, only that there is some love and affection between the spouses. In one case it was enough that the husband and wife were still living in the same home when the third party interfered with the marriage.[273] Also, all that needs to be established is the diminution of the affection, not that it was completely destroyed. Malice is established when the third party is aware of the marriage relationship and chooses to interfere—there is no need for the third party to harbor any ill will toward the innocent spouse. Finally, the fact that the plaintiff was also engaged in improper sexual conduct is not a defense to the tort.

This tort occurs in the state where the alienation occurs, even when the wrongdoer is in the state temporarily. For example, suppose that a South Carolina resident engages in an affair with a married person from South Carolinian—this tort is not recognized in South Carolina. The couple then decides to take a weekend trip to North Carolina, where the tort is recognized. The interfering party can be sued in North Carolina because some of the interference occurred on the weekend trip.

§16. Spoliation of Evidence

197. "Spoliation is the destruction or significant alteration of evidence, or the failure to preserve property for another's use as evidence in pending or reasonably foreseeable litigation."[274] The concept derives from the legal maxim "omnia praesumuntur contra spoliatorem," which when translated means all presumptions are against the depriver. Traditionally, this issue has been addressed at trial, usually with the judge sanctioning the person that destroyed or altered the evidence. More recently, some states have recognized a spoliation tort, independent of the original proceeding where the evidence could have been utilized. Where recognized, the tort can be against one of the parties to the original lawsuit (i.e., a first-party claim) or

273. *Nunn v. Allen*, 574 S.E.2d 35 (N.C. Ct. App. 2002).
274. *West v. Goodyear Tire & Rubber Co.*, 167 F.3d 776, 779 (2nd Cir. 1999).

against a nonparty (i.e., a third-party claim). A nonparty might include, for example, an insurance company that takes possession of a wrecked automobile and sells it for scrap before it can be inspected for defects. Of the states that recognize a spoliation tort, they tend to recognize it when the conduct is intentional rather than negligent. But a few do recognize negligence as well. The problem with this tort is the appropriate remedy. Assume, for example, that an insurance company negligently destroys evidence in a case where the damages to the plaintiff are millions of dollars. There seems to be some unfairness in assessing the insurance company for the entire amount of damages. Many states have yet to address this issue and the law is still developing.

§17. Tortious Interference with Inheritance

198. Nearly half of the states allow tortious interference with inheritance expectancy when third parties influenced testators to change their wills, retitle property, or change payable at death designations. This tort is disfavored because litigation is brought outside of the probate process, and states prefer all claims to be handled at one time by a probate judge—some states require exhaustion of the probate process before this tort can be brought. Most jurisdictions prohibit this tort completely. In one reported opinion, the caregiver of an elderly client was able to get the client to transfer all of her assets to her, and then name her as the sole beneficiary. When the client died, the caregiver waited several months before informing the family that their elderly relative had passed—she told them the day after the probate estate was closed and the probate court was unable to correct the fraud. This left the family with this tort as their only remedy, which the court allowed to proceed against the caregiver. *Schilling v. Herrera*, 952 So. 2d 1231 (Fla. Dist. Ct. App. 2007).

§18. Interference with Dead Bodies

199. This tort covers most of the improper actions that someone can do to a dead body, including unauthorized autopsies, embalming, cremation, mishandling, and withholding ashes. The conduct can be intentional, reckless, or negligent, and can be brought by the person who had the right to dispose of the body. A few states allow for the recovery of emotional harm for the mishandling of the remains of pets.

Chapter 3. Business Torts

200. Business torts primarily involve harm to commercial and economic interests, rather than harm to person or property. One characteristic of these torts is that they require the harmed party to prove pecuniary harm, which can be difficult given the cyclical nature of business profits.

§1. Fraudulent Misrepresentation

201. Fraudulent misrepresentation, referred to as deceit in common law, dates back to 1201 and allows for recovery of economic loss associated with a person's intentional falsehoods. Though initially limited to contractual claims, in 1789, fraudulent misrepresentation separated from contract and became an independent tort, thereby expanding the number of possible plaintiffs. Contractual claims are limited to those in privity—those who are part of the contract—while tort claims do not have the same limitation. Many jurisdictions have embraced the related tort of negligent misrepresentation while very few have adopted innocent misrepresentation (i.e., the strict liability version) because it is almost identical to express warranty in contract.

202. Not all lies that result in economic harm are protected, only those where there is a material misrepresentation by a person with knowledge of the false statement or an act in reckless disregard of the truth or falsity of the statement, intending to induce reliance, and the wronged party justifiably relies on the misrepresentation which results in pecuniary damages. If every misrepresentation was actionable the courts would be flooded with lawsuits; therefore, only those cases where all of the elements are established are actionable, but even then it is often difficult to win a fraudulent misrepresentation case.

203. Materiality is determined by what a reasonable person would attach importance to and will vary depending on the circumstances. For example, suppose that a stockbroker lies to a client about belonging to the same fraternal organization for the sole purpose of selling stock to the client, and a few days later the price of the stock goes down. A reasonable person would not find a sufficient connection between stock advice and membership in an organization unrelated to the stock. However, if the person making the misrepresentation knows that the person he is lying to attaches significance to the representation, then it can become a material misrepresentation. So if the lying stockbroker knows that the client only does business with other members of a particular fraternal organization, then that misrepresentation is material.

Only present and past facts can be misrepresented, and a present intention to not do something in the future is viewed as a present fact. Opinions are statements that cannot be subjected to truth or falsity, and therefore cannot create liability. Often opinions appear in the sales context where a salesman makes a comment like "that is a great car." In contrast, a statement by a salesman that "this car has a five-year manufacturer's warranty" is not an opinion but a fact. A material misrepresentation can occur without words, including the alteration of property to mislead someone. For example, a person that alters the odometer on a car is making a material misrepresentation to the person that purchases the car.

204. The final issue under material misrepresentation deals with the problem of silence. In other words, when will a person be held liable for not saying anything? The general rule is that one is under no duty to disclose material facts to another, but courts have begun to impose a duty in some areas. For example, in real-estate transactions, many states now require sellers to affirmatively disclose all material facts.

205. Fraudulent misrepresentation is an intentional tort where the person making the representation must know the representation is false or act in reckless disregard as to the truth or falsity of the representation. It is irrelevant that a reasonable person would have known that the statement is false since the test is what the person that made the representation intended (i.e., what they actually knew). As with most intentional torts, recklessness can act as a substitute for intent. Recklessness requires that the person making the misrepresentation be consciously aware of their lack of knowledge concerning the truth or falsity of the representation. For example, a potential home buyer asks the seller if the home is located in a specific school district. The seller then pretends to make a phone call, and after a few minutes responds that the house is in the desired school district. That is a purposeful act that disregards the truth or falsity of the representation.

206. A defendant is liable to all foreseeable plaintiffs where there was intent to induce reliance on the misrepresentation. A foreseeable plaintiff would include not only the person to whom the misrepresentation was made but also plaintiffs that the defendant likely knew would receive the misrepresentation. Strangers, at a train station or airport, who overhear a fraudulent misrepresentation, for example, would not be able to recover because there was no intent to induce reliance on them.

207. A defendant must be the actual and proximate cause of the plaintiff's reliance that results in a pecuniary loss. This does not mean that the defendant is required to be the sole cause but only a substantial cause in inducing reliance. In addition, reliance must have been justified. There is no requirement that a plaintiff acts as a reasonable person in the community, but a person's level of experience, qualities, and all of the circumstances will be examined in determining if their reliance on the misrepresentation was justifiable. Therefore, a fool's reliance on a fraudulent stock sale might be justified while a stockbroker's reliance might not. Under any circumstance, a person that knows that the representation is false will never be justified in relying on the representation.

208. Courts award damages using one of two approaches: the benefit of the bargain or out-of-pocket losses. Most courts allow the wronged party to collect the benefit of the bargain and calculate damages assuming that the representation had been true. A minority of courts allow out-of-pocket damages, which attempt to make the wronged party whole. A few courts allow the wronged party to choose one or the other damage, presumably allowing the greater amount. Finally, depending on the nature of the misrepresentation, punitive damages may be available.

§2. Negligent Misrepresentation

209. The definition of negligent misrepresentation is almost identical to that of fraudulent misrepresentation: there is a material misrepresentation by a person who negligently makes a false statement, intending to induce reliance, and the wronged party justifiably relies on the misrepresentation, which results in pecuniary damages. The primary issue in negligent misrepresentation is determining when a duty of care arises.

210. Courts are divided on determining when a duty of care exists, though generally there must be a special relationship between the plaintiff and the person making the representation. For example, a person relying on information supplied by their stockbroker expects the stockbroker to exercise ordinary care in preparing and communicating the information—a stockbroker that inadvertently tells a client that a share of stock is trending upward when it is actually trending downward, would be liable for negligent misrepresentation even though he did not intentionally or recklessly make a false statement.

211. A second important consideration involves the duty of care owed to third parties that rely on the misrepresentation. Liability is narrower for negligent misrepresentation than for fraudulent misrepresentation since not all foreseeable plaintiffs will be able to recover under negligent misrepresentation. New York was one of the first states to look at the issue and reject the idea that a negligent provider of information could have any duty to third parties. Most states however find that there is a duty to third parties when the negligent provider of information knows the identity of the third party and that the third party is going to rely on their representation. A few states have found that negligent information providers owe a duty of care to all foreseeable third parties.

§3. Intentional Interference with Contract and Intentional Interference with Prospective Economic Opportunity

212. A plaintiff with a claim for tortious interference with contract or interference with prospective economic opportunity must prove that a third party interfered with a valid contract or a prospective economic opportunity, had knowledge of the contract or prospective opportunity, acted intentionally, was unjustified, and caused the harm that led to pecuniary damages.[275] Because of the privity requirement in contract law, tort law is the only remedy that a person to a contract has against a third party that induces a breach of contract or interferes with a prospective business relationship. Though contract law does provide a remedy directly against the

275. *See Dykstra v. Page Holding Co.*, 2009 WL 1416119 (S.D. 2009).

breaching party, practically, that may not be viable when the breaching party does not have sufficient funds to cover a damage award. Also, tort damages in many jurisdictions are potentially greater than contract damages.

213. There must be a valid contract or viable prospective economic opportunity that the defendant interferes with. Interference with Contract protects the performance obligation of those in a contractual relationship while interference with economic opportunity protects those that are in a pre-contractual relationship. There is no liability if the contract is voidable, but there is liability for contracts terminable at-will if they have not been terminated.

214. The third party must either know that a contract exists or should know that a contract exists. There is no requirement that they know the exact terms of the contract. Likewise, with interference with economic opportunity, the third party must be aware or should be aware of the potential economic opportunity.

215. An interference is intentional if the consequence, the breach, is substantially certain to occur from the actor's actions. "The rule applies, in other words, to an interference that is incidental to the actor's independent purpose and desire but known to him to be a necessary consequence of his action."[276]

216. The third-party actor must be the actual and proximate cause of the breach. The key issue is whether the breaching party was in fact induced by the conduct of the third party. For example, a third party may attempt to induce breach by sending a letter to one of the contracting parties explaining that the other contracting party is bald. A breach of contract occurs but the breach has no relation to the letter attempting to induce breach and thus the third party is not the actual cause of the breach of contract.

217. Damages must be proven, with the following damages available: pecuniary, consequential, punitive, emotional distress, and reputational harm. For emotional distress and reputational harm, the damages must be reasonably expected by the interference. Punitive damages are available if the plaintiff can establish that the defendant acted with malice.

218. A contract may be interfered with if there is justification to do so. Some of the early cases noted that the defendant had to act with malice, but modernly this is understood as acting without justification or acting improperly. Acting improperly is when a defendant interferes using improper means or has an improper motive. Unfortunately, this area of the law is ambiguous, and impropriety is determined on a case-by-case basis. However, there is an agreement that the violation of a preexisting duty or an independent duty is improper, though this is not the only way to establish improper means or duty.

276. Restatement (Second) of Torts §766 cmt. j (1965).

219. States are divided on the question of which party is required to establish improper means or motive, or conduct. The more contemporary approach requires the plaintiff to establish this element as part of his prima facie case, while the older approach requires the defendant to raise it as an affirmative defense.

220. The United States Constitution's First Amendment prohibits this tort for nonviolent boycotts that are designed to further political, social, and economic change.[277] However, secondary boycotts are not protected by the Constitution. For example, individuals boycotting a hotel for their labor practices is a primary boycott and their actions are protected by the Constitution. But if those same individuals boycott a carpet seller because they are selling to the hotel, then that is a secondary boycott and that action is not protected by the Constitution.

§4. Tortious Breach of the Covenant of Good Faith and Fair Dealing

221. "Every contract imposes upon each party a duty of good faith and fair dealing in its performance and its enforcement."[278] The issue is whether this duty is one that will be enforced in contract or in tort, and if in tort then more generous tort damages—including punitive damages—become available. The courts have allowed tort suits involving breach of contract in two areas: third-party insurance and first-party insurance. The third-party insurance case involves a situation where an insurance company is representing its insured but is potentially liable for amounts in excess of the policy limits. If the insurance company fails to settle the claim in good faith then the insurance company may be sued by its insured for breaching its duty of good faith and fair dealing. The first-party insurance case involves a situation where the insurance company is providing first-party insurance to its insured (e.g., medical, fire, or theft). Courts have allowed tort actions to be brought by those that have had their claims denied in bad faith. In *State Farm Mut. Auto. Ins. Co. v. Campbell*, 538 U.S. 408 (2003), the Supreme Court of the United States decided a case involving a USD 145 million third-party insurance case, where the insurance company failed to settle the underlying claim for USD 50,000 when they had the opportunity to do so.[279] On remand based on due process constitutional grounds, the Utah courts reduced the punitive damage award to USD 10 million.

222. Attempts to expand this tort outside the insurance area have not fared well. California courts briefly allowed this type of tort action but quickly reversed course. A few states allow the action outside of the insurance context, but only under very limited circumstances.

277. *NAACP v. Claiborne Hardware Co.*, 458 U.S. 886 (1982).
278. Restatement (Second) of Contracts §205.
279. *State Farm Mut. Auto. Ins. Co. v. Campbell*, 538 U.S. 408 (2003).

§5. Breach of Fiduciary Duty

223. A breach of a fiduciary duty may result in tort liability. Fiduciary duties are imposed on agents acting for the benefit of a principal. Some fiduciary duties include the duty of loyalty, good faith, avoiding conflicts of interest, avoiding taking secret profits, confidentiality, and exercising due care.

224. A contract between the principal and agent can define the relationship between the parties, including the elimination of some fiduciary duties. For example, a fiduciary may not compete with the principal, but a contract may alter that to allow the fiduciary to compete. However, not all fiduciary duties can be altered. Generally, a fiduciary may not contract out of a duty of good faith. Also, it is difficult to contract out of duties when the principal is a corporation as those duties are generally imposed by law. Partnerships and limited liability companies are more flexible since the law allows them the freedom to contract, with very few restrictions.

§6. Economic Loss Rule

225. The economic loss rule prohibits tort lawsuits when a dangerously defective product causes stand-alone economic harm. When an unreasonably dangerous product causes harm, a plaintiff may recover damages under strict liability. But the economic loss rule is an exception to the general rule and requires the plaintiff to seek a remedy under contract law. Plaintiffs may prefer to sue in tort because of longer statutes of limitations or more generous remedies. Courts have reasoned that contract law is the proper arena for these claims because parties are free to contract for additional rights at the time of contract formation and a plaintiff should not later be able to receive more in tort when they were not willing to pay more for the product through an extended warranty.

226. For the economic loss rule to apply, the only injury must be to the product itself. If the dangerously defective product injures a person or other property then tort law may be used. A question that often arises involves the determination of what constitutes a product. For example, suppose that an automobile engine is dangerously defective and the car catches on fire, but only the car is damaged. Is the product the automobile or the defective engine? Courts use the economic loss rule to prohibit tort suits when a component in an integrated system causes stand-alone economic harm. But, if a plaintiff separately bargained for separate parts and a component part they integrated into a larger product causes economic harm to multiple components then the economic loss rule will not bar a tort action. For example, plaintiff decides to build his own automobile and purchases all the components separately. If the engine catches on fire and damages other car components, then the plaintiff may sue in tort and the economic loss rule will not bar the action.

§7. Injurious Falsehood

227. "Injurious falsehood" is a broad term that covers several torts that are all basically forms of defamation. Courts refer to these torts by the names of injurious falsehood, disparagement of property, slander of title, commercial disparagement, and trade libel. While defamation protects injury to reputation, injurious falsehood provides protection against harm to commercial and economic interests. To prove injurious falsehood, the plaintiff must establish that the defendant made a false statement with malice to another, with the likelihood that pecuniary harm would occur and in fact did occur. Malice is a technical term, meaning that the wrongdoer either knew the communication was false or acted with reckless disregard as to the communication's truth or falsehood. The false statement requirement can include any communication, including the filing of a lien or *lis pendens* regarding someone's property interest. While a false lien or *lis pendens* does not affect title to property, it can have the effect of keeping someone from purchasing the property.

§8. Prima Facie Tort

228. A few states, including New York, Missouri, and New Mexico, have adopted prima facie tort, which is a catch-all tort that captures harmful conduct that is not addressed by other torts. Prima facie tort occurs when there is an intentional lawful act, with an intent to injure the plaintiff, actual injury occurs, and there is an inadequate justification for the defendant's actions.

§9. Unfair Trade Practices

I. Federal

229. The Federal government has passed legislation making "unfair methods of competition in or affecting commerce, and unfair or deceptive acts or practices in or affecting commerce … unlawful."[280] Regulations are promulgated and enforced by the Federal Trade Commission. Because of the overlap between the federal law and state common-law actions, both are often pleaded in a lawsuit. A full discussion of the Federal Trade Commission Act is beyond the scope of this publication.

II. State

230. States have statutorily enacted consumer protection laws, which protect various activities depending on the state. As with the Federal Trade Commission Act, there is overlap with state common-law torts, resulting in plaintiffs pursuing

280. 15 U.S.C. §41(a)(1).

statutory and common-law remedies simultaneously. The phrase “unfair trade practice” is necessarily vague, which results in litigation to determine if a particular trade practice is or is not unfair.

Part II. Liability for Acts of Others

Chapter 1. Vicarious Liability

231. "Vicarious liability is liability for the tort of another person. Such liability is an important exception to the usual rule that each person is accountable for his own legal fault but in the absence of such fault is not responsible for the actions of others."[281] Most commonly, employers with no fault—arguably, innocent parties—may be held accountable for the torts of their employees through the doctrine of respondeat superior. The doctrine is not limited to the employer/employee context but also applies to independent contractors and volunteers.

The modern rationale supporting the doctrine is business enterprise liability, where a business is required to internalize all its costs—direct costs such as capital and labor, and indirect costs such as damages incurred in producing and marketing a product or service. Proponents of business enterprise liability explain that:

> the employee who commits a tort is usually judgment proof; if the injured person must look to the employee for reimbursement he will, as a practical matter, have no recourse at all. The employer, on the other hand, is more usually financially responsible; and since he knows of the liability for the torts of his servants, he can and should consider this liability as a cost of his business. He may avoid this cost by staying out of business entirely, or he can plan to carry such losses by insuring against them and adjusting his prices so that his patrons must bear part, if not all, of the burden of insurance. In this way losses are spread and the shock of accident is dispersed.[282]

It is this rationale—insurance coverage by business enterprises that spread the cost of tort injuries—that really drives the law of vicarious liability.

§1. Employee/Employer

232. Respondeat superior, an important concept under vicarious liability, is part of the law of Agency and is primarily focused on "the relations between principal and agent, principal and third person, and agent and third person."[283]"Agency is the

281. Dan B. Dobbs, *The Law of Torts* 905 (Thompson West 2000).
282. C. Morris, *The Torts of an Independent Contractor*, Ill. L. Rev. 29, 339, 340–341 (1934).
283. *See*, generally, Restatement (Second) of Agency SC NT (1958).

fiduciary relationship that arises when one person (a 'principal') manifests assent to another person (an 'agent') that the agent shall act on the principal's behalf and subject to the principal's control, and the agent manifests assent or otherwise consents so to act."[284]

Many cases and treatises use the older terms "master/servant" when dealing with respondeat superior, terms that are merely a type of principal/agent. Specifically, the master/servant relationship implies the principal's right of control over the servant's conduct. The modern trend is to replace master/servant with employer/employee—the change is probably due to egalitarian concerns in a society where few refer to their employer as "master." The Restatement (Third) of Agency, focusing on the control element in the principal/agent relationship, explains "an employee is an agent whose principal controls or has the right to control the manner and means of the agent's performance of work."[285]

233. The principles of Agency teach that employers are liable for the acts of their employees, with some limitations. Primarily, only employees acting within the scope of their employment can create liability for their employer. However, this principle has been interpreted broadly and is "much easier to state than to apply … ."[286] For example, in one case, a restaurant cook was talking to a customer while recklessly flipping a knife in the air. The knife injured the customer and the restaurant was held liable because the court held that the cook was acting within the scope of his employment when the knife injured the customer.[287] Even intentional, willful, or criminal acts are within the scope of the employment when there is a causal connection between the employee's position and the intentional, willful, or criminal conduct.[288] Going back to our knife-juggling cook for a moment, if the cook had deliberately stabbed his wife while he was on the job, he presumably would have done so outside the scope of his employment because employers are not liable for the unforeseeable intentional torts of their employees. Because of business enterprise liability courts have stretched the scope of the employment to capture activities that defy a common sense understanding of the phrase.

---

284. Restatement (Third) of Agency §1.01 (2006). Another definition for agency is "a fiduciary relationship created by express or implied contract or by law, in which one party (the agent) may act on behalf of another party (the principal) and bind that other party by words or actions." *Black's Law Dictionary*, 8th ed. (2004). The Restatement (Second) of Agency defines the terms as follows:

    1. Agency is the fiduciary relation that results from the manifestation of consent by one person to another that the other shall act on his behalf and subject to his control, and consent by the other so to act.
    2. The one for whom action is to be taken is the principal.
    3. The one who is to act is the agent. Restatement (Second) of Agency §1 (1958).

285. Restatement (Third) of Agency §7.07 (3)(a) (2006).
286. S.M. Speiser, C.F. Krause & A.W. Gans, *The American Law of Torts* §4:17 (Thompson-West 1983–2003).
287. *Riviello v. Waldron*, 391 N.E.2d 1278 (N.Y. 1979).
288. *Lisa M. v. Henry Mayo Mem'l Hosp.*, 907 P.2d 358, 361 (Cal. 1995).

234. This next statement may seem obvious, but employees must be working for their employer at the time they commit a tort to be within the scope of their employment. Therefore, employees that commit torts at home, on vacation, or commuting to or from work do not impute their actions to their employers through vicarious liability.[289] Yet once again we see courts willing to ignore this general rule and hold employers liable for employee conduct that occurs when employees are off the clock. A case in point involves an employee that was required to attend a sales convention in Alaska, where there were both business and social events. One evening, long after the business events were over, the employee drove from the convention center to a bar looking for his colleagues. When he did not find them, he drove back to the convention center. Unfortunately, his car collided with a pedestrian and he crushed the pedestrian's legs, resulting in the amputation of both legs. The accident, which occurred at 2:00 a.m., was found to be within the scope of his employment.[290] In another case, an employee was away from home supervising the opening of a restaurant for his employer. After midnight, several employees left work and went to a bar, where this employee drank four brandy Manhattans (including three doubles). This inebriated employee returned to his room around 1:30 a.m., began to fill out an expense report, and then fell asleep at a desk with a cigarette in his hand. The room caught on fire, causing severe damage to the motel. The motel successfully argued that the employee was acting within the scope of his employment, thereby holding the employer vicariously liable for the negligence of the employee.[291]

235. Finally, consider the case of the toll bridge company whose employee temporarily left his post and asked his son to watch the bridge in his absence. The son shot a man that crossed the bridge without paying the toll.[292] The court held that the son was an agent of the bridge company and that he was acting within the scope of his employment when he shot the nonpaying customer, even though the son was neither authorized to collect tolls nor paid for his services.[293] Case law shows this area to be exceptionally broad—employees invariably impute their negligence, and in some cases, their intentional or illegal acts, to their employers.

§2. Independent Contractors

236. An independent contractor is "one who is entrusted to undertake a specific project but who is left free to do the assigned work and to choose the method for

289. *Balise v. Underwood*, 428 P.2d 573, 577 (Wash. 1967). ("As a general rule, an employee traveling from the place of work to his home or other personal destination, after completing his day's work, cannot ordinarily be regarded as acting in the scope of his employment so as to charge the employer for the employee's negligence.").

290. *Fruit v. Schreiner*, 502 P.2d 133 (Alaska 1972). "[N]o categorical statement can delimit the meaning of 'scope of employment' once and for all times. Applicability of respondeat superior will depend primarily on the findings of fact in each case." *Ibid.*, at 141.

291. *Edgewater Motels, Inc. v. Gatzke*, 277 N.W.2d 11 (Minn. 1979).

292. *Ada-Konawa Bridge Co. v. Cargo*, 21 P.2d 1 (Okla. 1932).

293. *Ibid.*, 8.

accomplishing it."[294] Though the term is used with regularity by the courts, it is confusing and ambiguous because some independent contractors are agents while others are not. The labeling of a person as an independent contractor by an employer, even with the express consent of the employed person, is given little weight by courts, and substance of the relationship, not form, will be the controlling factor. Courts and administrative agencies make their own objective determinations as to whether an agency relationship exists—if the facts and circumstances indicate that the person is acting as an agent then courts use the respondeat superior rules and if the facts and circumstances indicate a true independent relationship then the rules for independent contractors apply. One definition reads:

> The most important test in determining whether a person employed to do certain work is an independent contractor or a mere servant or employee is the control over the work reserved by the employer .... Broadly stated, a contractor who is under the control of the employer is a servant, while one who is not under such control is an independent contractor.[295]

The Restatement (Third) of Agency abolishes the phrase independent contractor and focuses instead on whether a principal/agent relationship exists.[296]

237. With regard to the liability of general contractors or other principals for the torts of independent contractors, the general rule is that "the independent contractor's principal has no vicarious liability for the torts committed by the independent contractor or its employees in the performance of the contract."[297] The rationale for this general rule is that a principal contractor, unlike a direct employer, has little control over the actions of the independent contractor and thereby little power to prevent the occurrence of potential torts. Of course, a general contractor may still be held liable for the torts of independent contractors in certain circumstances. For example:

> Even if a contract clearly evinces the parties' settled intent to create a principal-independent contractor relationship, when a third party is adversely affected, this Court can look beyond the contract to determine whether public policy requires recharacterization of the relationship to allow the injured party to recover ....[298]

294. *Black's Law Dictionary*, 8th ed. (2004), 785.

295. 41 Am. Jur. 2d *Independent Contractors* §8 (2008).

296. Restatement (Third) of Agency §1.01 cmt. c (2006). "[T]he common term 'independent contractor' is equivocal in meaning and confusing in usage because some termed independent contractors are agents while others are nonagent service providers. The antonym of 'independent contractor' is also equivocal because one who is not an independent contractor may be an employee or a nonagent service provider. This Restatement does not use the term 'independent contractor', except in discussing other material that uses the term." *Ibid.*

297. *Chisolm v. Miss. Dept. of Transp.*, 942 So.2d 136, 141 (Miss. 2006) (citing *Heirs & Wrongful Death Beneficiaries of Branning ex rel. Tucker v. Hinds Cmty. Coll. Dist.*, 743 So.2d 311, 318 (Miss. 1999)).

298. *Ibid.* (citing *Richardson v. APAC-Mississippi, Inc.*, 631 So.2d 143, 150 (Miss. 1994)).

238. In addition to liability under modified applications of respondeat superior, a principal contractor can also be liable for the torts of its independent contractor under general negligence principles. Following the Restatement position:

> [a]n employer is subject to liability for physical harm to third persons caused by his failure to exercise reasonable care to employ a competent and careful contractor (a) to do work which will involve a risk of physical harm unless it is skillfully and carefully done, or (b) to perform any duty which the employer owes to third persons.[299]

The Restatement defines a "competent and careful contractor" as "a contractor who possesses the knowledge, skill, experience, and available equipment which a reasonable man would realize that a contractor must have in order to do the work which he is employed to do without creating unreasonable risk of injury to others."[300] For a party to succeed against the principal contractor under a negligence theory, they must prove "that the contractor was, in fact, incompetent or unskilled to perform the job for which he/she was hired, that the harm that resulted arose out of that incompetence, and that the principal knew or should have known of the incompetence."[301]

At this point there are so many exceptions to the general rule of no liability for the acts of an independent contractor, it might be better to explore those situations where an independent contractor does not create liability for their principal. As with employee torts, business enterprise liability is the rationale driving the expansion of liability for the torts of a principal's independent contractors.

§3. Liability of Legal Entities for Acts of Their Organs

239. The doctrine of respondeat superior applies to legal entities who by virtue of being nonpersons can only act through their agency relationship with others. In addition, when a director or principal of a corporation commits a tort, he may also be directly liable, both to the third party harmed and also potentially to the corporation itself. In a general partnership, each general partner is considered the partnership's agent and has apparent and actual authority to bind the partnership; as such, the liability for any tort committed by a partner within the scope of the agency relationship can be imputed to the partnership under general agency principles.

299. *Puckrein v. ATI Transport, Inc.*, 897 A.2d 1034, 1041–1042 (N.J. 2006) (citing Restatement (Second) of Torts §411 (1965); *Mavrikidis v. Petullo*, 707 A.2d 977 (N.J. 1998)).
300. *Puckrein v. ATI Transport, Inc.*, 897 A.2d 1034, 1041–1042 (N.J. 2006) (citing Restatement (Second) of Torts §411 (1965).
301. *Ibid.*

§4. VOLUNTEERS

240. A volunteer is a gratuitous agent that performs acts for a principal and can generally create tort liability for the principal, whether that principal is in the for-profit or nonprofit sector. Many of the reported cases over the last thirty years have occurred in the nonprofit sector, often with devastating effects on nonprofit organizations. In 2006, the Wisconsin Court of Appeals upheld a USD 18 million verdict—including USD 15 million for pain and suffering—against a nonprofit whose volunteer ran a red light, severely injuring an 82-year-old man.[302] The volunteer was a member of the Legion of Mary, located at a Roman Catholic Church within the Milwaukee Archdiocese. The Legion of Mary performed a number of activities, including “visiting families that … suffered a loss, visiting the parents of newborns, and … ” delivering statues of Mary. Because the nonprofit “controlled the activities and facilitates the mission of the Legion of Mary” the Court held the nonprofit vicariously liable for the actions of its negligent volunteer.[303] As with employees, nonprofits are held liable for the acts of volunteers when the nonprofit controls (or has the right to control) volunteers acting within the scope of their duties.

302. *Heikkinen v. United Serv. Auto. Ass'n*, 724 N.W.2d 243 (Wis. 2006).
303. *Ibid.*, 257.

Chapter 2. Liability of Parents, Teachers and Instructors (for Children, Minors, and Students)

241. The traditional American common law did not impose liability on parents for their children's torts. However, as the court system began to favor compensating innocent parties for harms they sustained at the hands of children, the courts began carving out exceptions to this general no-liability rule. Exceptions include when the parents ratify, direct, or encourage the child's tortious behavior, or when the child has otherwise acted as the parents' agent in the commission of the tort.[304] Louisiana, however, differs from all other United States jurisdictions and holds parents strictly and vicariously liable for the torts of their children.[305]

242. In addition to the above-mentioned exceptions, parents are also generally "under a duty to exercise reasonable care to control" their children so as to prevent them from causing harm to others.[306] The Second Restatement of Torts summarizes such liability as arising when "the parent knows or has reason to know (1) that he has the ability to control his child; and (2) of the necessity and the opportunity for exercising such control."[307] If a parent fails in performance of this duty, then he or she may be liable for the torts of the child, not under a theory of imputed liability, but under a theory of the parent's own negligence in failing to reasonably control the child so as to prevent the harm from occurring.[308]

243. Finally, many states have enacted statutes requiring parents to be responsible for a specific statutory amount when their children commit torts. The amounts tend to be fairly small and are not generally indexed for inflation.

304. *See*, e.g., *Hower v. Ulrich*, 27 A. 37 (Pa. 1893); *Trahan v. Smith*, 239 S.W. 345 (Tex. Civ. App. 1922); *Condel v. Savo*, 39 A.2d 51 (Pa. 1944).
305. *See* LSA C.C. Art. 2318 (1984).
306. *Reinert v. Dolezel*, 383 N.W.2d 148, 151 (Mich. Ct. App. 1985) (citing Restatement (Second) of Torts §315 (1965)).
307. Restatement (Second) of Torts §316 (1965).
308. *Ibid.*, §316 and comments.

Chapter 3. Liability for Things and Animals

§1. Livestock

244. The common law originally held livestock owners strictly liable for harm caused by their trespassing livestock.[309] Livestock cases generally involve cattle but might involve other animals that can be penned, such as sheep. State legislatures have, however, imposed statutes that in some cases have lessened the potential for strict liability and, in others, have returned to the common-law standard of strict liability for harm caused by trespassing livestock.[310] In addition, regardless of whether a particular state has reversed or continued the common-law strict liability standard, all states treat injuries caused by livestock on a public highway differently. In most jurisdictions, the owner of a livestock who wanders onto a highway is liable only for negligence;[311] however, a few jurisdictions would find that the livestock owner owes no duty at all to users of the highway and, as such, cannot be tortiously liable for harm.[312] As noted by one court:

> The historical rationale of the doctrine of strict liability for livestock trespass has largely been abandoned. The foundation of such liability currently is variously ascribed to defendant's possession and power of control of the animals, and the practical consideration that one raising livestock for his own use and profit should bear the burden and expense incident to their ordinary and predictable wanderings … Section 504, subdivision (1), of the Restatement of Torts purports to set out the common-law rule as follows: "(A) possessor of livestock which intrude upon the land of another is liable for their intrusion and for any harm done while upon the land to its possessor or a member of his household although the possessor of the livestock exercised the utmost care to prevent them from intruding." The law defining the scope of liability for trespassing livestock has been summarized by one authority as follows: "In general, strict liability has been confined to consequences which lie within the extraordinary risk whose existence calls for such special responsibility. Thus the owner of trespassing animals has been held strictly liable for consequences of the trespass which were reasonably to be expected from an invasion by animals of the particular kind-including, of course, damage to crops, attacks upon other animals, infecting them with disease, or the misalliance of a scrub bull with a pedigreed heifer. The same has been true of personal injuries suffered by the owner in an attempt to put the animal out, which has been regarded as foreseeable, reasonably likely to occur, and to provoke resistance. On the other

309. *Gravert v. Nebergall*, 539 N.W.2d 184, 186–187 (Iowa 1995) (citing *Wagner v. Bissell*, 3 Iowa 396, 401 (1856)).

310. *See Williams v. Goodwin*, 116 Cal. Rptr. 200, 205–208 (Cal. Dist. Ct. App 1974) (citing Prosser, *Law of Torts*, 4th ed. (1971), 496–503; Harper & James, *Law of Torts* (1956), 821–845; Restatement (Second) of Torts §504 and comments (1965)).

311. *Carrow Co. v. Lusby*, 804 P.2d 747, 751–752 (Ariz. 1990).

312. *See*, e.g., *Hitzel v. Clark*, 334 N.W.2d 37, 39 (S.D. 1983).

> hand, there are several cases denying recovery for injuries from quite unprovoked attacks, on the ground that they could not reasonably be expected to follow from the trespass .... In general, the cases support the view that the defendant will be liable only for normal consequences of the trespass, lying within the risk, which will vary with the type of animal involved, and may often be a jury question." ... We hold therefore that the infliction of personal injury by a bull upon an occupier of land, as the direct result of trespass by the bull upon that land, is within the scope of the risk of harm created by the trespass because it is obviously predictable and reasonably to be expected as a result of such a trespass. The rule expressed is consonant with the commonly acknowledged purpose of the application of strict liability to such cases, i.e., to allocate the burden of harm, in circumstances where damage of some sort is virtually inevitable, to the one having possession and control of the animal.[313]

§2. DOMESTIC ANIMALS

245. United States tort law has historically treated domestic animals (e.g., bees, cats, dogs, horses, mules, and some birds) differently than livestock. While there is no general rule imposing strict liability on the owners or keepers of domestic animals, liability may arise when the owner or keeper knows or has reason to know of an abnormally dangerous propensity of his domestic animal and when harm results from that danger.[314] The rule states:

> Strict liability attaches for harm done by a domestic animal where three elements are present: (1) one is the possessor of the animal, (2) one has scienter of the animal's abnormal dangerous propensities, and (3) the harm results from the dangerous propensity that was known or should have been known.[315]

Absent the presence of these three elements, the owner of a domestic animal is not strictly liable for harm caused by the domestic animal.

246. In addition, a domestic animal owner is not strictly liable for harm resulting from dangers that are normal to the species of animal they own. Normal dangers include aggressive bulls or frisky horses. The owner or keeper of these animals would not be strictly liable for harms resulting from those normal yet dangerous propensities "unless some added and abnormal quality" is proven.[316]

---

313. *Williams v. Goodwin*, 116 Cal. Rptr. 200, 205–208 (Cal. Ct. App 1974) (citing William Prosser, *Law of Torts* (4th ed. 1971). 496–503; Fowler V. Harper & Fleming James, *Law of Torts* (1956), 821–845; Restatement (Second) of Torts §504 and comments (1965)).

314. *Allen v. Cox*, 942 A.2d 296, 303–304 (Conn. 2008) (citing Restatement (Second) of Torts §509 and comments (1977)).

315. *Trager v. Thor*, 516 N.W.2d 69, 72–73 (Mich. 1994) (citing Restatement (Second) of Torts §509 (1977); *Knowles v. Mulder*, 41 N.W. 896 (Mich. 1889); *Kennett v. Engle*, 63 N.W. 1009 (Mich. 1895)).

316. *See*, e.g., *Duren v. Kunkel*, 814 S.W.2d 935 (Mo. 1991); *Jividen v. Law*, 461 S.E.2d 451 (W.Va. 1995).

§3. Wild Animals

247. Keepers of wild animals are strictly liable for the injuries caused by the animal, no matter how much care is exercised in preventing harm from occurring.[317] Although the law does not expressly define what constitutes a wild animal, the definition is not confined to animals that are universally considered violent or highly dangerous; rather, an animal is considered wild when it is not, by local custom, devoted "to the service of mankind at the time and in the place in which it is kept."[318] Even when a keeper claims to have tamed a wild animal, he is not relieved of strict liability "for damages caused by such animal. Such a rule would be contrary to both reason and authority."[319] Strict liability, on the other hand, is often rejected for zoos and is also generally limited to harms that result from "a dangerous propensity that is characteristic of wild animals of the particular class, or of which the possessor knows or has reason to know."[320] Some courts have held the following animals to be wild: bears, coyotes, leopards, lions, monkeys, and snakes.

§4. Defenses

248. The available defenses would depend on the cause of action. Generally though, comparative fault is the primary defense available. *See* discussion below of Strict Liability defenses under Part III, Chapter 2 and Negligence under Part IV, Chapter 3.

§5. Liability of a Thing

249. Liability of things is not recognized in the United States. A person that is negligent or intentional in placing a thing in a certain location might be held liable, but that is because of their conduct. The ancient Germanic concept of holding a thing liable for its own fault when it injures someone is not recognized.

317. *See*, e.g., *Poznanski ex rel. Poznanski v. Horvath*, 788 N.E.2d 1255, 1259 (Ind. 2003) (citing *Irvine v. Rare Feline Breeding Ctr., Inc.*, 685 N.E.2d 120, 125 (Ind. Ct. App. 1997)).
318. *Lineberry v. Riley Farms Prop. Owners Ass'n*, 236 S.W.3d 534, 538 (Ark. Ct. App. 2006) (citing Restatement (Second) of Torts §506 (1977)).
319. *Newman v. Cleveland Museum of Natural History*, 55 N.E.2d 575, 579 (Ohio 1944).
320. *Irvine v. Rare Feline Breeding Ctr., Inc.*, 685 N.E.2d 120, 125 (Ind. Ct. App. 1997) (citing Restatement (Second) of Torts §507 (1977)).

Part III. Forms of Strict Liability

Chapter 1. Road and Traffic Accidents

250. Most jurisdictions have not enacted specific civil tort laws to deal with road and traffic accidents, and strict liability would generally not be applicable to these types of injuries. The negligence per se doctrine, discussed above, is broad enough to cover negligent road and traffic accidents. While negligence per se can be viewed as a type of strict liability, negligence per se still focuses on the actor's conduct while strict liability focuses on the activity of the actor.

Chapter 2. Products Liability

§1. Overview

251. Products liability developed as a tort action encompassing the reasons for and the defenses to manufacturer and seller liability for injuries caused by unreasonably dangerous products or products that are not reasonably safe for their intended uses.[321] Products liability claims may be brought under one of four causes of action: negligence, warranty, strict liability, or misrepresentation, though all four may not be available to a plaintiff in every jurisdiction.[322] Originally, the concept of manufacturer liability arose under contract law and warranty principles and, as such, required privity between buyer and seller to proceed. But over time the action sounded more in tort than contract, with the privity requirement gradually abolished.[323] The overriding principle that remains in all modern products liability actions, whether sounding in strict liability, negligence, warranty, or misrepresentation, is that liability turns on whether the plaintiff can prove the defective nature of the product.[324] Whether a product is defective will rely on one of three theories as to the nature of the defect—manufacturing defect, design defect, or warning defect.

§2. Defective Product

I. Three Types of Defects

252. American products liability law imposes liability for three categories of product defects: manufacturing, design, and warning defects. A plaintiff may bring one or more of four causes of action and then argue that the product was defective using one or more theories as to the nature of the defect. States are divided on what causes of action are available in their states, with a few states completely rejecting strict products liability.

253. A manufacturing defect, also called a manufacturing flaw, is a random imperfection in a product that unexpectedly departs from that product's intended design in such a way as to make it unreasonably dangerous.[325] It is not a defect that runs throughout an entire product line but is an isolated defect in a specific item, as in the classic example of the rare exploding soda bottle. Throughout most of the twentieth century, soda bottles were returned to manufacturers, who reused the bottles after testing them for flaws. In some rare instances, these bottles exploded in the hands of customers. An exploding piece of glass is unreasonably dangerous and

321. *Azzarello v. Black Bros. Co., Inc.*, 391 A.2d 1020, 1023–1026 (Pa. 1978).
322. *See*, e.g., *Sternhagen v. Dow Co.*, 935 P.2d 1139, 1143–1144 (Mont. 1997); *Johnson v. Chrysler Corp.*, 254 N.W.2d 569, 571 (Mich. Ct. App. 1977).
323. *See Azzarello v. Black Bros. Co., Inc.*, 391 A.2d 1020, 1023–1024 (Pa. 1978) (discussing the development of product liability law and the abolishment of the privity requirement).
324. *See*, e.g., *Doe v. Solvay Pharmaceuticals, Inc.*, 350 F.Supp.2d 257, 266 (D.Me. 2004).
325. *Ford Motor Co. v. Ledesma*, 242 S.W.3d 32, 41–42 (Tex. 2007).

is usually due to a manufacturing defect since soda bottles are made to withstand normal use. To prove a manufacturing defect, a plaintiff must show: "(1) the product deviated from its specifications or planned output in a manner that rendered the product unreasonably dangerous; (2) the defect existed at the time the product left the possession of the defendant; and (3) the defect was a producing cause of the injury."[326]

254. Unlike a manufacturing defect, which occurs in isolation within a product line, a design defect is a defect in the intended design of a product that renders the entire product line unreasonably dangerous.[327] To prove a design defect, "a plaintiff must show that (1) there was a defect in the product manufactured and sold by the defendant, (2) the defect existed at the time the product left the defendant's control, and (3) the defect was the direct and proximate cause of the plaintiff's injuries or losses."[328] For example, if a car manufacturer intentionally manufactured all of its automobiles without seat belts that would likely be viewed as a design defect because it would be unreasonably dangerous to sell cars without this important safety feature.

255. A warning or instruction defect exists when a product becomes unreasonably dangerous because it fails to provide potential hazard warnings or adequate instructions. If the warnings or instructions had been provided, the product would not have been unreasonably dangerous. The Restatement is informative on the subject of warning defects:

> One who supplies directly or through a third person a chattel for another to use is subject to liability to those whom the supplier should expect to use the chattel with the consent of the other or to be endangered by its probable use, for physical harm caused by the use of the chattel in the manner for which and by a person for whose use it is supplied, if the supplier (a) knows or has reason to know that the chattel is or is likely to be dangerous for the use for which it is supplied, and (b) has no reason to believe that those for whose use the chattel is supplied will realize it's dangerous condition, and (c) fails to exercise reasonable care to inform them of its dangerous condition or of the facts which make it likely to be dangerous.[329]

Most jurisdictions recognize that "a manufacturer has the duty to warn ultimate users of its products or articles which are inherently dangerous or are dangerous because of the use to which they are put. The duty to warn for foreseeable and latent

326. *Ibid.*
327. *Smith v. Brown & Williamson Tobacco Corp.*, 275 S.W.3d 748, 792–793 (Mo. Ct. App. 2008).
328. *Donegal Mut. Ins. v. White Consol. Indus., Inc.*, 852 N.E.2d 215, 220 (Ohio Ct. App. 2006).
329. *Smith v. Brown & Williamson Tobacco Corp.*, 275 S.W.3d 748, 784–785 (Mo. Ct. App. 2008) (citing Restatement (Second) of Torts §388 (1965)).

dangers is attendant to the proper and intended use of a product … ."[330] If a plaintiff establishes that he did not know of the product's danger, then a rebuttable presumption arises that he would have heeded a warning or followed an instruction if one had been provided.[331]

II. Obvious Dangers

256. While a manufacturer has a duty to warn of dangers that are unknown to the users of its product, a manufacturer has no duty to warn of any dangers that "are within the ordinary common knowledge of the community" or are otherwise obvious risks.[332] This no-duty-to-warn requirement has come to be known as the "open and obvious doctrine" and serves as an affirmative defense in a failure-to-warn claim.[333] As explained by the Wisconsin Court of Appeals, a manufacturer's:

> duty to warn depends … on whether the supplier or manufacturer has reason to believe the user will realize the danger involved … [A] supplier or manufacturer has no duty to warn of a danger is when "a mere casual looking over will disclose [the dangerous condition] unless the circumstances under which the chattel is supplied are such as to make it likely that even so casual an inspection will not be made." When danger is obvious from a mere casual looking over, the supplier or manufacturer has reason to believe that the user will realize the danger.[334]

A Michigan court opined:

> In the context of warnings of the obvious danger of simple products, the duty inquiry asks whether people must be told what they already know. Warnings protect consumers where the manufacturer or seller has superior knowledge of the products' dangerous characteristics and those to whom the warning would be directed would be ignorant of the facts that a warning would communicate. Thus, it has been observed that no duty exists to warn users of its products when "the consumer is in just as good a position as the manufacturer to gauge the dangers associated with the product … ." A manufacturer cannot manufacture a knife that will not cut or a hammer that will not mash a thumb or a stove that will not burn a finger. The law does not require [a manufacturer] to warn of such.[335]

An example from the Restatement illustrates the point:

330. *Ibid.*, 785.
331. *Brown & Williamson Tobacco Corp.*, 275 S.W.3d 785.
332. *Painter v. Momentum Energy Corp.*, 271 S.W.3d 388 (Tex. App. 2008) (citing *Joseph E. Seagram & Sons, Inc. v. McGuire*, 814 S.W.2d 385, 388 (Tex. 1991)).
333. *Mohr v. St. Paul Fire & Marine Ins. Co.*, 674 N.W.2d 576, 587 (Wis. Ct. App. 2003) (citing Restatement (Second) of Torts §388(b) and cmt. k (1965)).
334. *Ibid.*
335. *Glittenberg v. Doughboy Recreational Indus.*, 491 N.W.2d 208, 213 (Mich. 1992).

XYZ Ladder Co. manufactures kitchen step ladders for home use. Sid used an XYZ ladder to post a sign above the door of his home office, unaware that his five-year-old son was playing in the office. While Sid was standing on the ladder, his son suddenly opened the door, which struck the ladder. Sid fell off the ladder and suffered a fractured hip. There were no warnings on the ladder, nor in the instruction booklet that came with it, not to use the ladder in front of an unlocked door. The danger should be obvious to foreseeable product users. No reasonable trier of fact would find XYZ liable for failing to warn about it and the court should rule for XYZ as a matter of law.[336]

III. Causation (Unforeseeable Misuse)

257. A product is only defective if the harm sustained was reasonably foreseeable to the manufacturer before it left the manufacturer's control.[337] A plaintiff's unforeseeable misuse of a product which leads to harm negates an element of the prima facie products liability claim if the unforeseeable misuse was a superseding event that broke the causal connection between any alleged product defect and the resultant harm.[338] On the other hand, foreseeable misuse is not actually true misuse and does not contradict a product's defectiveness.[339] For example, toaster manufacturers know that consumers often place pieces of bread that are larger than the normal size sold in grocery stores in toasters. A toaster that catches on fire because an oversized piece of bread causes a fire is a foreseeable misuse of the toaster—the manufacturer would be the proximate cause of the injury. But a piece of cold meat placed in a toaster is an unforeseeable misuse, and thus the manufacturer is not the proximate cause of the injury.

IV. Persons to Be Warned

A. Allergic or Idiosyncratic User

258. United States jurisdictions differ in their treatment of allergic users in products liability warning claims. The states that adhere to a risk-utility analysis on the adequacy of a warning analyze whether the manufacturer should foresee the allergy and, if so, the gravity of the allergic reaction compared to any associated costs of warning the user, in determining whether a warning is required.[340] Other states adhere to a rule based on the potential for harm to the majority of users in the manufacturer's market in determining whether a warning is required and not requiring a

336. Restatement (Third) of Torts: Prod. Liab. §2 (1998) (Illust. 12).
337. *Atkins v. Gen. Motors Corp.*, 725 N.E.2d 727, 732 (Ohio Ct. App. 1999).
338. *See*, e.g., *Collins v. Li*, 933 A.2d 528, 580 (Md. 2007).
339. *Dreyer v. Exel Indus., S.A.*, 326 Fed. Appx. 353, 356–357 (6th Cir. 2009).
340. *Advance Chemical Co. v. Harter*, 478 So.2d 444 (Fla. Dist. Ct. App. 1985) (citing 2 R.D. Hursh & H.J. Bailey, *American Law of Products Liability* §12:4 (2d ed., 1974)); *Seller's or Manufacturer's Liability for Injuries as Effected by Buyer's or User's Allergy or Unusual Susceptibility to Injury from Article*, 26 A.L.R.2d 963 (1952)).

warning for rare cases of adverse reaction, no matter how severe the reaction.[341] For example, Illinois courts analyzed the issue of the allergic or idiosyncratic user based on other jurisdictions' analyzes and concluded that:

> if the product does not threaten severe harm to the ordinary consumer, then it is reasonably fit for the purpose for which it is sold. The benefit to the mass public who use the product is said to outweigh the harm suffered by the insignificant few. The proximate cause of injury is attributed to the idiosyncrasy or allergy of the plaintiff and not to a failure to warn of a defect in the product.[342]

B. Professional User

259. Professional users are treated differently from ordinary consumers, such as:

> [W]here a product is used in an industrial setting by one supposedly skilled at his job, a manufacturer has no duty to warn of dangers inherent in the task or which are created by oversight or negligence of the contractor or fellow employees. Moreover, a manufacturer is entitled to assume that professional users of its product will heed its warnings, and is not required to foresee that professional users will fail to read its warnings, then use the product in a manner that the manufacturer's instructions expressly warned against.[343]

C. Post-sale Duty to Warn

260. Although there is no consensus among the states for post-sale warnings by manufacturers, the majority of jurisdictions impose some duty on manufacturers to inform or warn purchasers of their products of hazards discovered after the manufacture or sale of their goods, including the discovery of better safety technology.[344] This post-sale imposed duty is generally based on a risk-utility analysis: knowledge by the manufacturer or seller of the newly discovered danger, whether the gravity of the danger is greater than the burden to warn, and whether a post-sale warning can effectively reach the product user.[345] But this post-sale duty does come to an end. For example, a company that sold an item in 1920 would not have a duty today to warn of new safety features. Presumably, this is because any failure to warn would begin to accrue at the time the item was sold, and thus any post-sale duty would end at the time the statute of limitation expires.

---

341. *See*, e.g., *Payne v. Soft Sheen Prods., Inc.*, 486 A.2d 712, 722 (D.C. 1985).
342. *Presbrey v. Gillette Co.*, 435 N.E.2d 513, 520 (Ill. App. Ct. 1982) (citations omitted).
343. *Basford v. Gray Mfg. Co., Inc.*, 11 P.3d 1281, 1285 (Okla. Civ. App. 2000) (citations omitted).
344. *See*, e.g., *Lewis v. Ariens Co.*, 751 N.E.2d 862, 866–867 (Mass., 2001).
345. *Ibid.*

§3. Causes of Action

I. Strict Liability

261. The most useful form of products liability, from the plaintiff's perspective, is strict liability. It is the most plaintiff-friendly cause of action because the focus is on the product and not on the conduct of the manufacturer. The focus of a strict liability claim is around two issues: is there a defective product that is unreasonably dangerous? First adopted by California in 1963 in products liability cases, the Restatement Second of Torts quickly followed suit and adopted §402A—its version of strict products liability.[346] Within a decade, most states had adopted strict products liability. Some of the rationales for allowing strict liability are as follows:

1. strict liability will spread the cost of the loss around by manufacturers incorporating such risks into the price of their products;
2. strict liability will deter unsafe products and lead to increased product safety; and
3. manufacturers implicitly warrant the safety of their products to their users.[347]

Recently there has been some movement away from strict liability in design defect and failure-to-warn cases by the Third Restatement of Torts, which has eliminated all references to strict liability for products liability actions.[348] The Restatement does not have the force of law, but it is extremely persuasive in moving the courts in its direction.

A. Establishing a Defect

262. The first step in a products liability case is determining whether a defect exists in the product, either because of a manufacturing defect, design defect, or warning defect. Of the three types of defects, a manufacturing defect is probably the one that plaintiffs will have the easiest time proving. Most products liability cases require the use of expert witnesses, but courts will generally allow proof of manufacturing defects without the need for experts. After all, if a product is missing parts, it will be difficult for the manufacturer to argue that the item was sold as it was intended to be sold. The more difficult issue is proving that the defective product was also unreasonably dangerous.

263. Design defect cases are those where the plaintiff concedes that the product was sold exactly as the manufacturer intended to sell the product, but that the design of the product is the defect and that the product could have been produced using a safer alternative. Proving that there was a safer alternative design will require the

346. *Greenman v. Yuba Power Prods., Inc.*, 377 P.2d 897 (Cal. 1963).

347. *See Lunsford v. Saberhagen Holdings, Inc.*, 106 P.3d 808, 812 (Wash. Ct. App. 2005) (citing Restatement (Second) of Torts §402A cmt. c (1965)).

348. *See*, generally, Restatement (Third) of Torts (1998).

use of experts, leading to plaintiff's expert arguing that there was a safer design and the defendant's plaintiff arguing that the product was designed as safely as it could at the time it was manufactured.

264. Failure-to-warn cases involve inadequate instructions or inadequate warnings on foreseeable uses of the product. Most courts also add that failure to warn encompasses foreseeable misuse of the product. For more complicated products experts might be needed to establish the exact nature of the defect, but for most products, juries are competent to decide failure-to-warn cases without the need for expert testimony.

265. In determining whether a defect exists, states employ the consumer-expectation test, the risk-utility test, or a combination of the two. A majority of states however use some version of the risk-utility test.

266. With the rapid adoption of strict products liability in the 1960s, courts were faced with creating tests that could be used in determining if a product was unreasonably dangerous. The Restatement Second of Torts §402A did not provide a test, but the consumer-expectation test was suggested in the comments section and adopted by many states. The Restatement (Third) Torts notes that it does not endorse an independent consumer expectations test, though it recognizes that the analysis in the consumer-expectation test can resemble a risk-utility analysis. The consumer-expectation test is explained as follows:

> A product is "unreasonably dangerous" due to a defect in either manufacturing or design when it is "dangerous to an extent beyond that which would be contemplated by the ordinary consumer who purchases it, with the ordinary knowledge common to the community as to its characteristics." We further stated that in a strict products liability action, a claim of defective design may be proven in either of two ways. First, the plaintiff may introduce "evidence that the product failed to perform as safely as an ordinary consumer would expect when used in an intended or reasonably foreseeable manner." This has come to be known as the consumer-expectation test.[349]

267. The second and more common test is the risk-utility test. For states that use this test, arguably they have moved away from strict liability and reintroduced negligence principles into products liability. As one court explained the test:

> the plaintiff may introduce "evidence that the product's design proximately caused his injury." If the defendant thereafter "fails to prove that on balance the benefits of the challenged design outweigh the risk of danger inherent in such designs," the plaintiff will prevail. This test, which added the balancing

---

349. *Mikolajczyk v. Ford Motor Co.*, 901 N.E.2d 329, 335–336 (Ill. 2008) (citing *Lamkin v. Towner*, 563 N.E.2d 449 (Ill. 1990)).

of risks and benefits to the alternative design and feasibility inquiries … has come to be known as the risk-utility or risk-benefit test.[350]

Only a few states use a pure risk-utility test, with most states incorporating both the risk-utility and consumer-expectation tests into their law.

B. Establishing Unreasonable Danger

268. To prevail in a products liability case, the plaintiff must establish that the product was unreasonably dangerous. "A product may be found to be unreasonably dangerous based on proof of any one of three conditions: a physical defect in the product itself, a defect in the product's design, or a failure of the manufacturer to warn of the danger or to instruct on the proper use of the product."[351] The following illustrates this point:

> XYZ Corp. designs and markets a new television antenna for home use that utilizes the electrical system in the buyer's home as the main signal receptor. The new antenna improves reception compared with traditional television antennas, but also introduces significant risks of electrical shock and electrocution. XYZ markets the new antenna with warnings about these risks, and emphasizes the benefits of improved reception to be derived from using the electrical wiring system. Fred buys one of the new antennas and installs it in his home. Two months later Fred suffers serious electrical burns while changing channels on his television set. Fred brings an action against XYZ, claiming that the design of the new television antenna is defective. At trial, Fred relies on the availability of traditional television antennas that are not connected with electrical systems to show that reasonable alternative designs could have been adopted by the manufacturer. In connection with proving that the defendant's design is defective … Fred is not confined to offering variations of television antennas that rely on electrical wiring systems. The feature of XYZ's design that presents the risk of electrocution—incorporating preexisting electrical wiring systems—is merely a means of achieving the objective of improved television reception. That feature does not, in itself, provide consumers with intrinsic benefits other than its effects on reception. Merely because the defendant chooses to emphasize that feature in its marketing does not prevent the plaintiff from proving that the increases in risk generated by that feature more than outweigh any increases in reception when compared with traditional antenna systems.[352]

350. *Ibid.*
351. *Ibid.* (citing *Sollami v. Eaton*, 772 N.E.2d 215 (Ill. 2002)).
352. Restatement (Third) of Torts: Prod. Liab. §2 (1998) (Illust. 8).

C. Status of Seller

1. Retailers and Wholesalers

269. All sellers in the commercial chain are liable under strict liability, including the manufacturer, wholesaler, and retailer. Even those sellers that are not in the business of selling the product that caused the harm are liable under strict liability. For example, "the owner of a motion picture theater who sells popcorn or ice cream, either for consumption on the premises or in packages to be taken home" is strictly liable for injury caused by the popcorn or ice cream.[353] This rule ensures that an injured plaintiff will likely recover damages. The question of who should bear the cost among the possible defendants can be handled by contract before a lawsuit or in a contribution action after the products liability lawsuit. In other words, a retailer that in no way was at fault for the defect will likely be able to recover from the manufacturer of the product.

2. Sellers of Used Products

270. Used product sellers are generally not liable under strict liability. But sellers of used products may be held strictly liable when the used seller leads a buyer to reasonably believe that the used product is not more dangerous than a new product, the used product is remanufactured, or the used product fails to meet a safety guideline or statute. For example:

> ABC Motor Parts Co. sells both new and remanufactured replacement parts. ABC sold Alice a remanufactured fuel pump for her 1994 Blazer Sedan. XYZ Rebuilders, Inc. remanufactured the fuel pump and sold it to ABC. Alice paid 25% less for the remanufactured fuel pump than a new fuel pump would have cost. Shortly after installation of the remanufactured fuel pump Alice's car stalled while making a turn in an intersection. A collision ensued causing serious injury to Alice. Alice's expert presents credible testimony that a bracket in the fuel pump dislodged and blocked the flow of fuel and that the bracket was defectively assembled by XYZ. Both ABC and XYZ are subject to liability without fault for the harm caused by the defect.[354]

3. Lessors

271. Lessors can be held strictly liable for the lease of unreasonably dangerous products. This seems, at first blush, like an odd result because a lessor is not selling anything. As leases have become more common and in some cases look similar to

353. Restatement (Second) of Torts §402A, cmt. f (1965).
354. Restatement (Third) of Torts: Prod. Liab. §8 (1998) (Illust. 18).

a sale, courts have been willing to hold lessors of goods strictly liable.[355] But it is unlikely that financial lessors (i.e., those that merely provide leasing finance) will be held strictly liable for physical injury resulting from defective products.[356]

D. Defenses

272. A plaintiff's comparative fault may reduce the amount of damages they may recover in most states that have adopted strict products liability, although a few states retain an express assumption of the risk as a complete defense. For a full discussion of defenses, *see* Part IV, Chapter 3 below.

II. Negligence

273. Though strict liability is the most favored cause of action, negligence remains a viable option, especially in states that do not recognize strict products liability. The elements of negligence, as fully explained above in Part I, Chapter 2, §10, are duty, breach of duty, actual cause, proximate cause, and harm.

Manufacturers, wholesalers, and retailers owe a duty of reasonable care to purchasers or those that are injured by the product. In most products liability cases, the primary problem is establishing a breach of duty because there is often no evidence to establish unreasonable conduct. For example, in a manufacturing defect case, it may be impossible to discover what unreasonable conduct led to a missing part in a product sold by a manufacturer. As to wholesalers and retailers, they generally act as conduits and will practically never be held liable for negligence, unless they were aware of the defect and failed to take reasonable steps to stop selling the defective product.

274. Res ipsa loquitur is a doctrine that is used when there is a lack of direct evidence needed to establish breach of duty.[357] The phrase means "the thing speaks for itself" and provides the fact finder with a means for considering circumstantial evidence. When res ipsa loquitur applies, a jury may infer that the defendant breached their duty of reasonable care. In one case, res ipsa loquitur was allowed when a commercial airplane mysteriously crashed and there was no evidence of unreasonable conduct.[358] But commercial airplanes, in the modern era, do not fall out of the sky absent negligence or intentional conduct. To use res ipsa loquitur a plaintiff must establish that event that caused the harm does not normally occur without negligence and that the defendant was likely responsible for the negligence—if those tests are met the jury may infer breach of duty. But with some products, it may be difficult to prove that the defendant was likely negligent. For

355. *Crowe v. Public Bldg. Comm'n of Chicago*, 383 N.E.2d 951 (Ill. 1978).
356. *Abco Metals Corp. v. Equico Lessors, Inc.*, 721 F.2d 583 (7th Cir. 1983).
357. This Latin phrase was introduced into the law of torts in *Byrne v. Boadle*, 2 H. & C. 722, 159 Eng. Rep. 299 (Exch. 1863).
358. *Widmyer v. Southeast Skyways, Inc.*, 584 P.2d 1, 13 (Alaska 1978).

example, suppose that a glass bottle explodes in someone's hand. Did the manufacturer create the defect or was it negligent handling of the bottle by the wholesaler or retailer? Res ipsa loquitur can therefore be useful in some negligence cases.

275. As discussed below in Part V, a plaintiff needs to establish actual cause, proximate cause, and harm. One potential issue is the proximate cause question of who is a foreseeable plaintiff—should anyone injured by the product recover or only those that were foreseeable at the time the product was sold? For example, suppose a manufacturer sells a product that may only be legally used in certain regulated laboratories. If the product is stolen and purchased by a good faith purchaser, should that purchaser be able to sue the manufacturer if they are injured? Finally, how should damages be apportioned if there were several manufacturers that helped to produce the product? These are difficult questions that are left to the jury to resolve.

III. Warranty

A. *Overview*

276. A warranty cause of action is partly tort and partly contract. It is part contract because it arises from the contractual obligations created by the buyer and seller, or contractual obligations imposed by the Uniform Commercial Code. The Uniform Commercial Code is model legislation that has been adopted by almost every state. Warranty is also part tort because of the harm that occurs when the product operates in a defective manner. Prior to the widespread adoption of strict products liability, warranty actions were common but could be difficult to win because of the limitations that contract law imposed on the actions—problems with privity, ability to disclaim liability, and available damages. Today warranty is the third most common cause of action in a products liability case after strict liability and negligence. In the landmark case from California, *Greenman v. Yuba Power Products, Inc.*, Justice Traynor reasoned that a tort case should not depend on the particulars of warranty.[359] However, in states that have not adopted strict products liability, warranty is the most common cause of action and in most states, plaintiffs may still choose to bring this cause of action. Plaintiffs may choose to bring a warranty action when they suffered a pure economic loss. The economic loss rule, discussed above in Part I, Chapter 3, §6, does not allow for the recovery of stand-alone economic loss, but a warranty action may allow for economic damage recoveries, such as lost business profits or other consequential damages.

277. There are three types of warranty actions: express warranty, implied warranty of merchantability, and implied warranty of fitness for particular purpose. Because they are contractual in nature they are strict liability actions (i.e., there is no need to prove intent or fault to prevail). Before the middle of the twentieth century, one problem that plaintiffs encountered was the privity requirement, which limited actions to the buyer and seller. The Uniform Commercial Code provides

359. *Greenman v. Yuba Power Prods., Inc.*, 377 P.2d 897 (Cal. 1963).

states with three privity alternatives that they can adopt, ranging from less restrictive to more restrictive, with most states adopting the alternative that is least restrictive and therefore allows more injured people to sue under warranty.[360] But even these restrictions have been eased by some states, either judicially or by statute so that all foreseeable plaintiffs will generally be able to sue under warranty and all defendants in the commercial chain can be potentially liable.

B. Express Warranty

278. The Uniform Commercial Code provides four methods for establishing an express warranty: affirmation of fact or promise, description of goods, a sample, or a remedial promise.[361]

To bind the seller, the express warranty must precede the sale or occur at the time of sale, and the warranty may be oral or written. A seller's opinion is not considered a promise and does not bind the seller—a seller's opinion is commonly referred to as "puffing." For example, a seller that claims that his product is the best in its class is puffing and does not create an express warranty. In addition to the express warranty, the Uniform Commercial Code requires that the warranty must also be the basis of the bargain, which is a matter for the fact finder to determine in litigation.

C. Implied Warranty of Merchantability

279. The Uniform Commercial Code provides "a warranty that the goods shall be merchantable is implied in a contract for their sale if the seller is a merchant with respect to goods of that kind."[362] Goods are merchantable if they at a minimum:

---

360. Uniform Commercial Code, §2-318 (amend. 2003).

361. *Ibid.*, §2-313 (amend. 2003). Express Warranties by Affirmation, Promise, Description, Sample; Remedial Promise:

1. In this section, "immediate buyer" means a buyer that enters into a contract with the seller.
2. Express warranties by the seller to the immediate buyer are created as follows:
    a. Any affirmation of fact or promise made by the seller that relates to the goods and becomes part of the basis of the bargain creates an express warranty that the goods shall conform to the affirmation or promise.
    b. Any description of the goods that is made part of the basis of the bargain creates an express warranty that the goods shall conform to the description.
    c. Any sample or model that is made part of the basis of the bargain creates an express warranty that the whole of the goods shall conform to the sample or model.
3. It is not necessary to the creation of an express warranty that the seller use formal words such as "warrant" or "guarantee" or that the seller have a specific intention to make a warranty, but an affirmation merely of the value of the goods or a statement purporting to be merely the seller's opinion or commendation of the goods does not create a warranty.
4. Any remedial promise made by the seller to the immediate buyer creates an obligation that the promise will be performed upon the happening of the specified event.

362. Uniform Commercial Code, §2-314(1) (amend. 2003).

a. pass without objection in the trade under the contract description;
b. in the case of fungible goods, are of fair average quality within the description;
c. are fit for the ordinary purposes for which goods of that description are used;
d. run, within the variations permitted by the agreement, of even kind, quality and quantity within each unit and among all units involved;
e. are adequately contained, packaged, and labeled as the agreement may require; and
f. conform to the promise or affirmations of fact made on the container or label if any.[363]

280. What the courts look for in a product is one that is reasonably safe, not one that is perfect. This warranty runs with all goods that are sold, though this implied warranty can be limited or disclaimed. Finally, a plaintiff may only sue a merchant that sells these types of products. For example, a store that sells motorcycles can be sued for a defective motorcycle, but a used bookstore owner that sells his motorcycle out of his store is not a merchant for implied warranty of merchantability purposes.

D. Implied Warranty of Fitness for Particular Purpose

281. The provision for the implied warranty or fitness for particular purpose from the Uniform Commercial Code states:

> Where the seller at the time of contracting has reason to know any particular purpose for which the goods are required and that the buyer is relying on the seller's skill or judgment to select or furnish suitable goods, there is … an implied warranty that the goods shall be fit for such purpose.[364]

First, this provision only deals with goods used for a particular purpose and not goods that are used as intended. The product is not defective when used as intended, but becomes defective when used for the buyer's particular purpose. Second, the buyer must actually rely on the seller's skill or judgment when they buy the product they are going to use for their particular purpose. For example, a person walks into a lawn mower shop and explains to the clerk that they want a lawn mower capable of cutting grass and very small trees growing on his property. Normally lawn mowers are not used for cutting small trees but the seller directs the buyer to a very powerful lawn mower that he believes will do the job. If the buyer is injured by the lawn mower then he may maintain an action for this implied warranty. Unlike the implied warranty of merchantability, there is no requirement that the seller be a merchant.

363. *Ibid.*, §2-314(2) (amend. 2003).
364. *Ibid.*, §2-315 (amend. 2003).

E. Warranty Disclaimers

282. One of the primary reasons many states adopted strict products liability was because all warranties, express or implied, can be limited or completely disclaimed. Disclaimers make perfect sense under contract law because contract law is concerned with promoting bargaining freedom among individuals. But that rationale is at odds with tort law, which is concerned, primarily, with making an injured person whole. The relevant provision reads:

(2) Subject to subsection (3), to exclude or modify the implied warranty of merchantability or any part of it in a consumer contract the language must be in a record, be conspicuous, and state "The seller undertakes no responsibility for the quality of the goods except as otherwise provided in this contract," and in any other contract the language must mention merchantability and in case of a record must be conspicuous. Subject to subsection (3), to exclude or modify the implied warranty of fitness, the exclusion must be in a record and be conspicuous. Language to exclude all implied warranties of fitness in a consumer contract must state "The seller assumes no responsibility that the goods will be fit for any particular purpose for which you may be buying these goods, except as otherwise provided in the contract," and in any other contract the language is sufficient if it states, for example, that "There are no warranties that extend beyond the description on the face hereof." Language that satisfies the requirements of this subsection for the exclusion or modification of a warranty in a consumer contract also satisfies the requirements for any other contract.

(3) Notwithstanding subsection (2):
  - (a) unless the circumstances indicate otherwise, all implied warranties are excluded by expressions like "as is," "with all faults" or other language that in common understanding calls the buyer's attention to the exclusion of warranties, makes plain that there is no implied warranty, and, in a consumer contract evidenced by a record, is set forth conspicuously in the record;
  - (b) if the buyer before entering into the contract has examined the goods or the sample or model as fully as desired or has refused to examine the goods after a demand by the seller there is no implied warranty with regard to defects that an examination in the circumstances should have revealed to the buyer.[365]

The disclaimer must be conspicuous to the extent that a reasonable person should have noticed it. This is an objective test that is left for the court, not the jury to decide. The court will examine the font, the surrounding text, whether all capitals were used, different colors, or special marks that were used to bring attention to the disclaimer.[366]

---

365. *Ibid.*, §2-316 (amend. 2003).
366. *Ibid.*, §2-103(1)(b) (amend. 2003).

F. Notice

283. One significant requirement under the Uniform Commercial Code is that the injured party provides notice to the seller of the defective product within a reasonable amount of time and allows a breaching party to cure the problem.[367] Failure to provide notice may bar the plaintiff's recovery. While this notice requirement makes sense for commercial buyers and sellers, it is unlikely that a person injured by a defective product is going to be aware of this provision. Courts are sensitive to this problem and have generally allowed lawsuits to continue, even in cases where years have passed from the time the plaintiff became aware of the defective product.

IV. Misrepresentation

284. Misrepresentation can arise when a seller represents a false fact concerning a product. For a full discussion of misrepresentation, *see* Part I, Chapter 3, §§ 1 and 2. Fraudulent misrepresentation is the most common type, followed by negligent misrepresentation, and then innocent misrepresentation. Though innocent misrepresentation is generally not accepted by most states, it is accepted in products liability to deal with the problem of false advertising. Innocent misrepresentation is the strict liability version of the tort—the seller does not need to know of the false fact nor should they have known of the false fact and is very similar to Express Warranty.

285. The elements of innocent misrepresentation include (1) a false representation of material fact; (2) the intent to induce reliance; (3) justifiable reliance; and (4) damages. The Restatement Second defines it as:

> One engaged in the business of selling chattels who, by advertising, labels, or otherwise, makes to the public a misrepresentation of a material fact concerning the character or quality of a chattel sold by him is subject to liability for physical harm to a consumer of the chattel caused by justifiable reliance upon the misrepresentation, even though
> (a) it is not made fraudulently or negligently, and
> (b) the consumer has not bought the chattel from or entered into any contractual relation with the seller.[368]

Though innocent misrepresentation is similar to Express Warranty, there are two important differences. First, there is no requirement that the plaintiff provide the defendant with notice to allow the defendant to cure the defect. Second, a defendant cannot argue that they disclaimed the representation.

367. *Ibid.*, §2-607(3)(a) (amend. 2003).
368. Restatement (Second) of Torts, §402B (1965).

Chapter 3. Liability for Service

286. Pure service providers are not liable under strict liability because they are not sellers of products. Also, repairers of products are not generally liable under strict products liability.[369] But a repairer may be liable in their capacity as a seller of a defective product that they used in making the repair. A few states have extended liability to hybrid service providers—those that sell goods along with services. In *Newmark v. Gimbels, Inc.*, the defendant went to a beauty salon and requested a service to make her hair curly. The hair stylist placed defective hair products in her hair that caused a burning sensation and her hair to fall out. The court explained that the stylist was engaged in a commercial enterprise and would therefore be held liable under strict liability.[370]

369. *Levine v. Sears Roebuck and Co.*, 200 F.Supp.2d 180 (E.D.N.Y. 2002).
370. *New Mark v. Gimbel's, Inc.*, 258 A.2d 697 (N.J. 1969).

Chapter 4. Environmental Liability

§1. Nuisance

287. A nuisance occurs when a person interferes with the property rights of another individual (i.e., private nuisance) or the public (i.e., public nuisance). Though related to property law, nuisance is properly a tort because it involves injury, which does not have to be physical, occurring either to people or property, while property law is concerned with determining the rights in property between two or more parties. Courts use theories of negligence, strict liability, and intent in establishing a nuisance, but defenses usually available in those areas are not available when the court labels the action as a nuisance. Trespass to land is a related tort but differs from nuisance in that a trespass is generally of a more permanent nature or involves a more tangible intrusion. For example, a rock thrown onto another's land is a trespass because rocks are tangible and are permanent unless moved, but smoke blowing onto another's land is a nuisance because smoke is not tangible and quickly dissipates.

288. Remedies for a nuisance include money damages or an injunction. American law favors the award of money damages over an injunction, but if the nuisance is of a continuing nature then the courts will exercise their equitable powers and grant an injunction.

289. A person with a current possessory property interest may institute a private nuisance action when there is an unreasonable interference with his use or enjoyment of the property. A number of states have divided private nuisances into two types: *nuisance per se* and *nuisance per accidens*. A *nuisance per se* is an interference that is always a nuisance regardless of the circumstances, while a *nuisance per accidens* is an interference that under some circumstances substantially interferes with plaintiff's comfortable enjoyment. For example, noxious odors wafting from another's property is a *nuisance per se*, while a high-frequency pitch only heard by dogs that cause them to bark would be a *nuisance per accidens* only to those that own dogs.

290. Only those with a current possessory interest in the land have standing to sue under private nuisance. This could include an owner or tenant, but the key is determining those that have the right to exercise physical control over the land. For example, a person staying in a hotel room for a few days would likely not have a sufficient possessory interest in the land, just like a guest in another's summer cottage would not have a possessory interest in the land.

291. What qualifies as an unreasonable interference will depend on the circumstances, but courts often look at the time, place, magnitude, and duration of the interference. For example, a few hours of smoke emanating from a barbeque at a personal residence is not a nuisance, but that same smoke billowing into another yard eight hours a day seven days a week is a nuisance.

292. A public nuisance occurs when there is an unreasonable interference with a right enjoyed by the public in the use of public spaces. Examples of public spaces include roads, streams, parks, and the ocean. Proper plaintiffs include the government or a private plaintiff with a special injury. A special injury is one that is not common to the entire public and one that has caused direct economic harm to the plaintiff. Often these special injury plaintiffs are commercial fishermen that bring public nuisance actions for pollution in some bodies of water, resulting in a reduction in the number of available fish and therefore a harm to the fishermen's livelihood. The more remote the harm the less likely that the plaintiff will prevail.

§2. Environmental and Zoning Laws

293. A portion of what can be brought under nuisance, especially public nuisance, is often also regulated by federal and state laws. At the state level, zoning laws may dictate what a person may do with their property, and at the residential level, it is common for there to be covenants between homeowners regulating property usage. Federal and state environmental laws provide the government with additional tools in preventing unreasonable discharges of hazardous materials into the air, ground, or water.

Chapter 5. Others

§1. Abnormally Dangerous Activities

294. Those that engage in abnormally dangerous activities are strictly liable for physical harm they cause. An abnormally dangerous activity—sometimes referred to as an ultra-hazardous activity—is one that is not of common usage and one that creates a foreseeable and highly significant risk of harm. Because strict liability focuses on the nature of the activity and not conduct, a person that exercises due care or even the highest level of care will be liable when harm occurs. A truck carrying nitroglycerin explodes, injuring a person in another car, is an example of engaging in an abnormally dangerous activity. However, the harm that occurs must be the type of harm expected to occur by engaging in an abnormally dangerous activity. For example, a truck carrying gasoline, a highly flammable liquid, leaks a large quantity of gasoline on the road. An automobile drives into the gasoline and slides into a ditch. The truck driver is not liable under the abnormally dangerous activity doctrine because the foreseeable risk of harm for gasoline is flammability, which did not occur under these facts. The injured driver however would be able to bring a negligence claim.

295. The traditional defense to abnormally dangerous activity is the assumption of the risk. A person assumes a risk when they fully understand the risk and voluntarily assumes the risk of harm. With the adoption of comparative fault in most American jurisdictions, a few courts have allowed defendants to use comparative fault as a partial defense to an abnormally dangerous activity claim. *See* Part IV, Chapter 3 for a discussion of defenses.

Part IV. Defenses and Exception Clauses

Chapter 1. Limitation of Action (Suspension and Interruption)

296. All torts are governed by statutes of limitations, which impose a time limit during which a cause of action can be brought. Any cause of action brought after the expiration of the statute of limitation, even if only by a single day or because of a good faith mistake, will be procedurally barred. All states have their own statutes of limitations, with differing time periods depending on the cause of action.

297. Usually, the statute of limitation begins to run at the time the tortious act occurs, but there are often exceptions for continuing torts or torts that are not discovered at the time they occur. A continuing tort is one where a defendant fails to stop some prior action or continues in a particular course of action. For example, a factory that sends toxic fumes into the air and refuses to stop the pollution. The question is whether the tortious conduct occurred on the first day the factory polluted or did each day of pollution start the statute of limitation clock anew. Courts answer this question differently depending on the circumstances. Another continuous tort situation occurs when the person that committed the original tort attempts to work with the injured party before litigation to remedy the problem. The issue here is whether the statute of limitations begins to run on the day of the injury or at the time the relationship between the two parties is terminated. For example, a doctor misdiagnoses a patient's cancer but agrees to treat the patient for free—this treatment could last for years, extending beyond the statute of limitation. The law favors tortfeasors that attempt to right the wrong, therefore the statute of limitation will generally be deemed to have begun at the end of the treatment and not at the first act of tortious conduct.

298. A second exception to the statute of limitation is the Discovery Rule, where a person is harmed but is unaware of the harm at the time it occurs. A common example involves the negligent surgeon that leaves a medical implement inside a patient after surgery. Under the Discovery Rule, the statute of limitation is extended until the time that the plaintiff becomes aware of the injury or should have become aware of the injury. Going back to the surgery example, if one week after the surgery the patient feels a cold piece of metal inside his body cavity then that begins the statute of limitation, even though he may not get an x-ray for several years—he should have known that negligence occurred at the point he felt the metal, even though he may not have known for certain until he saw the x-ray.

299. Stolen personal property presents some interesting problems because it might be decades before the original owner, or his heirs, locate the property. Cases in this area often involve artwork stolen by the Nazis and found by heirs many years later, usually in the hands of a good faith purchaser. Though most states apply their normal statute of limitations, a few states, including New York, have allowed the original owner to recover stolen property from a bona fide purchaser decades after the theft. New York avoids the statute of limitation problem by imposing on the original owner a "demand and refusal requirement," where the statute begins to run on the date that the owner's demand for the return of the property is refused by the bona fide purchaser.[371]

300. The need for finality has caused states to create statutes of repose—a final date after which no action can be extended. A common statute of repose limits exceptions like the Discovery Rule to ten years after the date of the original tortious conduct. Courts determine the date when the original tortious conduct occurred, which begins both the statute of limitation and the statute of repose.

371. *Kunstsammlungen Zu Weimar v. Elicofon*, 678 F.2d 1150 (2d Cir. 1982).

Chapter 2. Grounds of Justification for Intentional Torts

§1. Consent

301. In most circumstances, consent is a complete defense to an intentional tort and the plaintiff is privileged in committing the tort. It is an affirmative defense and therefore the defendant has the burden of proving the defense. Consent can be in writing or provided orally, and can be express or implied. There is no particular form in which consent is given, but it must be objectively manifested by the defendant. For example, defendant owns a doll that plaintiff believes is hideously ugly and plaintiff asks for permission to destroy the doll. Defendant expressly consents to the destruction of the doll but secretly wants to say no. Express consent was properly given based on the defendant's objective manifestation. However, if plaintiff was aware of defendant's subjective denial of consent then there is no valid consent because defendant knew that consent was not actually being granted. An objective observer with all of the facts would not have burned the doll, so there was no consent.

302. Consent may be implied based on all surrounding circumstances. For example, a person agrees to be on a reality television show where they know they will be placed on an island with other contestants for a week. That person has impliedly consented to be on the island and therefore the plaintiff was privileged to commit the tort of false imprisonment. Consent may also be implied by law. Often this occurs in medical emergencies when the injured party cannot give consent. An example might include a person found unconscious in an automobile wreck, who is given blood to keep them alive. Unknown to the physician that gave them the blood the injured person had religious beliefs prohibiting blood transfusions. This doctor is not liable for battery because the law implies that people want to live rather than die. But, if the unconscious person was wearing identification negating consent to a blood transfusion, then the physician cannot claim the defense.

303. Consent may be invalidated under certain circumstances. Fraud that induces someone to improperly give consent can be invalidated at the option of the person that granted consent. Actions that are outside of the scope of consent may be invalidated. For example, a person playing football consents, at least impliedly, to some physical contact. But a punch to the face is outside of the scope of consent granted in football. Incapacity can be used to invalidate consent, such as when a young child agrees to get into a stranger's car or when a person with insufficient mental capacity agrees to sell their house at a bargain price. Duress is another time when consent may be invalidated. Finally, most American courts hold that consent cannot be granted for illegal acts.

§2. Necessity

304. There are two types of necessity defenses: private and public. A private necessity is a defense that allows one person to interfere with the property rights of another, but it is an incomplete defense in that the interfering person must compensate for any damages they cause. In one famous case, a person was sailing on a lake when a storm suddenly arose. The boat moored onto a private dock but the owner of the dock untied the rope, causing damage to the boat. The dock owner was required to compensate the boat owner because the boat owner was privileged to keep his boat on the dock until danger had passed.[372] Some authority holds that the danger must be imminent and serious.

305. A public necessity is a complete defense and allows the appropriation of private property when there is a great public need. Most of the public necessity cases involve appropriation of private property during natural disasters, raging fires, and war when the enemy is about to enter a city. The appropriation can occur by government officials or private individuals, depending on the circumstances. If there is a time of public necessity then neither the party that takes another's property nor the government is responsible for compensation. During the Japanese invasion of the Philippines, the United States Army destroyed oil facilities to keep them out of enemy hands. The Supreme Court of the United States held that there was a public necessity that the United States Army was privileged to destroy the property, and therefore there was no need to compensate the refinery owner, even under the Takings Clause of the United States Constitution.[373] More recently, some state courts have found that the government is responsible for compensating those whose property is taken during a public necessity because cost should be borne by all of society, not individual property owners.

§3. Self-Defense

306. A person is privileged to use reasonable force in self-defense of their person when an attack is imminent, though the privilege cannot be used to justify a preemptive strike. Reasonable force occurs when the amount of force used is proportionate to the amount of force being used against them. In addition to acting reasonably, the person claiming the defense must also subjectively believe that force is necessary for the protection of their body. Thus, the defense has both a subjective and objective component.

307. Force sufficient to kill another is privileged only when the other person is about to inflict serious physical harm or deadly force. For example, when someone is about to kick another the person about to be kicked may not use a knife to stop the kick since that is disproportionate. But if a person is about to be stabbed then he may use a gun to shoot the other person.

308. A majority of American jurisdictions hold that there is no duty to retreat from an imminent attack, even if one can safely do so. Even when the only alternative is to use deadly force, there is no duty to retreat. A minority of jurisdictions

372. *Ploof v. Putnam*, 81 Vt. 471, 71 A. 188 (Vermont 1908).
373. *United States v. Caltex, Inc.*, 344 U.S. 149 (1952).

require retreat if it can be accomplished safely, though even these jurisdictions do not require retreat from one's own home.

§4. Defense of Others

309. An intervener is privileged in using force to help another against a third party when the intervener reasonably believes that the person he is helping is privileged to defend himself. For example, person X notices two people, Y and Z, fighting each other. X reasonably believes that Y is the instigator, so X uses reasonable force to stop Y. X may claim the defense of the other's privilege. This is a modern departure from the traditional rule, which placed the intervening person in the position of the person they were helping (i.e., one stands in the same shoes as the person that could have claimed self-defense). Thus, under the traditional rule, the intervener cannot claim the privilege if they make a reasonable mistake.

310. This is an area of law where there has not been much litigation and most of the authority supports the traditional rule. However, in the criminal context, the rule was changed decades ago to one that allows a person to intervene if he reasonably believes he is helping the person that was privileged to do so. It is unlikely that many jurisdictions dealing with this issue today would follow the traditional rule though the law, in cases decided before the 1960s, supports the traditional rule.

§5. Defense and Recovery of Property

311. Defense of property is available when a person uses reasonable force to protect his property. Generally what is reasonable will depend on the circumstances, though a rule of proportionality is often used. For example, if X is about to take Y's property, X should first command Y to stop. Under no circumstances may a person use deadly force or force intended to inflict serious bodily harm to protect property. If deadly force is the only means that can be used to protect property then the property must be forfeited and the theft reported to the police.

312. Because of the high value placed on human life, property owners are not allowed to use mechanical devices or traps likely to inflict death or serious bodily harm to protect their property. In one case a property owner was tired of people trespassing in the abandoned home of his deceased mother. The owner placed a shotgun in a room, set to shoot the leg of anyone entering the room. A trespasser entered the room and one of his legs was almost destroyed. The trespasser sued under battery and the property owner argued that he was privileged in defending his property. The court held that a property owner is not privileged to use deadly force or force likely to inflict serious bodily harm when property is the only thing being protected. Thus the trespasser was able to recover damages from the property owner.[374]

374. *Katko v. Briney*, 183 N.W.2d 657 (Iowa 1971).

313. While a reasonable mistake is allowed under defense of others, reasonable mistakes are not tolerated for those defending their property—one invades the interests of another at the risk of being sued for false imprisonment or battery. This can be particularly challenging for merchants, who want to detain potential shoplifters. By statute many states now allow merchants to use reasonable force to detain suspected shoplifters for a reasonable amount of time.

§6. Automatism

314. Automatism, commonly called sleepwalking, negates the intent element of an intentional tort when the defendant establishes that they were not awake at the time the tort occurred. All intentional torts require voluntary action, and thus the argument that one is not awake at the time the tort has the effect of establishing that the action was involuntary and therefore not intentional. For example, a known sleepwalker is seen burning another's home. If he was asleep at the time that he burned the house, his action was involuntary and not intentional. The defendant is required to prove that he was sleepwalking.

§7. Brainwashing (Stockholm Syndrome)

315. The brainwashing defense—the purposeful effort to change the will of another without their consent and then to force them to commit an act they would not voluntarily have committed—has not been successful. The most famous attempt at using the defense involves Patty Hearst, who was kidnapped in 1974 by an organization attempting to start a revolution in the United States. After a period of captivity, she joined the group and helped to rob a bank. Her defense at trial was that she had been, effectively, brainwashed after enduring severe physical and emotional harm by her captors. Psychologists are not generally in agreement that Stockholm Syndrome exists as a psychological disorder.

Chapter 3. Contributory Fault

§1. CONTRIBUTORY NEGLIGENCE

316. Contributory negligence is "an affirmative defense that must be proved according to an objective standard whether the plaintiff failed to act as a reasonable person would have acted for his or her own safety under the circumstances."[375] Under the traditional rule, contributory negligence served as a complete bar to the plaintiff's claim, even if the plaintiff was only minimally negligent compared to the defendant.[376] Because of its harsh effects, especially for the extremeness that results in cases of significantly disproportionate degrees of negligence, comparative negligence has replaced contributory negligence in all but five U.S. jurisdictions (Alabama, Virginia, Maryland, North Carolina, and the District of Columbia).[377] In those states, however, the rule still acts as an absolute defense to a plaintiff's negligence claim.

317. General negligence refers to one's failure to exercise due care with respect to the welfare of others, while contributory negligence refers to one's failure to exercise due care for one's own welfare.[378] This doctrine does not serve to relieve the defendant of any duty owed to the plaintiff but is premised on the notion that a plaintiff cannot recover for harm caused to him by another party if he also took part in causing that harm to himself. Under the doctrine of contributory negligence, if the person injured by the tortfeasor contributes in any way to his own injury, he cannot recover anything from the tortfeasor. This is true even when the injured person is less than 1% at fault. Whether a plaintiff has been contributorily negligent is generally a question of fact to be decided by a jury.[379]

318. One exception to the contributory negligence rule is the "last clear chance" doctrine, though it only applies in those few states that retain contributory negligence. Under this exception, even if a plaintiff is contributorily negligent, he can still recover if the defendant had the last clear chance to avoid the accident and failed to do so. One court explained the rule as follows:

> [T]he doctrine of last clear chance permits a contributorily negligent plaintiff to recover damages from a negligent defendant if each of the following elements is satisfied: (i) the defendant is negligent; (ii) the plaintiff is contributorily negligent; and (iii) the plaintiff makes a showing of something new or

---

375. *Fultz v. Delhaize America, Inc.*, 677 S.E.2d 272, 275 (Va. 2009).
376. S. Gardner, *Contributory Negligence, Comparative Negligence, and Stare Decisis in North Carolina*, Campbell L. Rev. 18, 1, 2 (1996).
377. *Ibid.*
378. *Ibid.*, 7–8.
379. *Fultz v. Delhaize America, Inc.*, 677 S.E.2d 272, 275 (Va. 2009) (citing *Moses v. Southwestern Va. Transit Mgmt. Co.*, 643 S.E.2d 156, 159–160 (Va. 2007)).

sequential, which affords the defendant a fresh opportunity (of which he fails to avail himself) to avert the consequences of his original negligence.[380]

In these situations, the rationale for permitting the plaintiff to recover despite his contributory negligence is that "if the defendant has the last clear opportunity to avoid the harm, the plaintiff's negligence is not a proximate cause of the result."[381] As such, the last clear chance doctrine only applies when the defendant has time to act to avoid harming the plaintiff after the plaintiff's own negligence and still causes said harm. Concurrent acts of negligence by the plaintiff and defendant do not implicate this exception.[382]

319. In addition, a modification of the last clear chance doctrine is the discovered peril rule, in which courts only apply the last clear chance exception to the contributory negligence bar when the plaintiff proves the following elements: "(i) the defendant is negligent; (ii) the plaintiff is contributorily negligent; and (iii) the plaintiff makes 'a showing of something new or sequential, which affords the defendant a fresh opportunity (of which he fails to avail himself) to avert the consequences of his original negligence.'"[383] Under this modification, the last clear chance exception only applies when the defendant discovers plaintiff's perilous position and had the ability and opportunity to avoid the resultant harm but failed to do so.

§2. Assumption of the Risk

320. The second traditional affirmative defense in negligence is the assumption of the risk, which is basically equivalent to the consent defense in intentional tort cases and acts as a complete bar to recovery. While contributory negligence employs an objective test, assumption of the risk uses a subjective test—did the plaintiff appreciate the risk of harm and voluntarily choose to assume the risk? There are two types of assumptions of risk: express and implied. A plaintiff may, orally or in writing, disclaim the defendant's potential liability for a risk of harm that the plaintiff understands and voluntarily assumes. For example, plaintiff decides to go whitewater rafting and signs a form explaining that death or serious bodily harm may occur. If the contemplated risk occurs then express assumption of the risk bars the plaintiff from recovery. As to implied assumption of the risk, most courts no longer consider it as a separate defense and instead examine a person's subjective implied assumption of the risk under comparative fault rules. Even express assumption of the risk is increasingly being considered under comparative fault rules rather than as a separate defense. The thought for the merging of assumption of the risk with comparative fault is that juries will allocate more fault to a person that assumes the risk of harm.

---

380. *Wooldridge v. Price*, 966 A.2d 955, 961 (Md. 2009) (citing *Burdette v. Rockville Crane Rental, Inc.*, 745 A.2d 457 (Md. 2000)).
381. *Ibid.*
382. *Ibid.*
383. *Ibid.* (citing *Burdette v. Rockville Crane Rental, Inc.*, 745 A.2d 457 (Md. 2000)) (quoting *Liscombe v. Potomac Edison Co.*, 495 A.2d 838 (Md. 1985)).

§3. Comparative Negligence

321. Most American jurisdictions have moved away from contributory negligence and assumption of the risk, and have adopted principles of comparative fault. Rather than a plaintiff's contributory negligence completely barring his recovery, comparative negligence would reduce any potential recovery to the plaintiff proportionally based on his level of fault.[384] This same principle of apportionment applies when multiple defendants are involved, assigning liability to each party based on each party's proportionate fault in the harm.

I. Pure Comparative Negligence

322. Pure comparative negligence apportions a plaintiff's comparative fault in all negligence cases, regardless of which party is most at fault.[385] A minority of the jurisdictions that operate under comparative negligence have adopted this version. For example, under pure comparative negligence principles, even a plaintiff that is 95% at fault for an accident may recover 5% of the damages from the defendant.

II. Modified Comparative Negligence

323. Modified comparative negligence is a compromise position somewhere[386] in-between pure comparative negligence and traditional contributory negligence with its absolute bar to the plaintiff's recovery. Specifically, under modified comparative negligence, once a plaintiff's fault reaches a certain percentage, they are completely barred from recovery. Modified comparative negligence operates under three slight variations: the not-greater-than version, the less-than-or-equal-to version, or the slight/gross version. Under the not-greater-than version, if a plaintiff is more at fault than the defendant, then they are completely barred from recovery. Twenty-one states follow the not-greater-than version of the doctrine. Under the less-than-or-equal-to version, if the plaintiff's fault is equal to the fault of the defendant, then he cannot recover, but if his fault is only 49% compared to the defendant's 51%, then he can recover that 51% from the defendant. Eleven states follow the less-than-or-equal-to rule. The third adaptation of modified comparative negligence is the slight/gross rule, which allows recovery by the plaintiff for the defendant's "gross fault if the plaintiff's fault is slight in comparison."[387]

384. *See*, e.g., *Aguallo v. City of Scottsbluff*, 678 N.W.2d 82, 90 (Neb. 2004).

385. S. Gardner, *Contributory Negligence, Comparative Negligence, and Stare Decisis in North Carolina*, Campbell L. Rev. 18, 1, 33–34 (1996).

386. *Ibid.*, 33–35.

387. *Ibid.*, 35.

Chapter 4. Exemptions

§1. Immunities

I. Overview

324. Through most of the twentieth century, all immunities were either limited or abolished.

II. Charitable Immunity

325. Charities no longer enjoy immunity for their tortious conduct. There was a time when charities did enjoy a judicially created immunity, but today only a few states still retain some form of charitable immunity.[388] However, the federal government has enacted the Volunteer Protection Act, which provides immunity to the volunteers of charities if certain conditions are met:

1. the volunteer … [must have been] acting within the scope of the volunteer's responsibilities in the nonprofit organization or governmental entity at the time of the act or omission;
2. if appropriate or required, the volunteer … [must have been] properly licensed, certified, or authorized by the appropriate authorities for the activities or practice in the State in which the harm occurred, where the activities were or practice was undertaken within the scope of the volunteer's responsibilities in the nonprofit organization or governmental entity;
3. the harm … [must not have been] caused by willful or criminal misconduct, gross negligence, reckless misconduct, or a conscious, flagrant indifference to the rights or safety of the individual harmed by the volunteer; and
4. the harm … [must not have been] caused by the volunteer operating a motor vehicle, vessel, aircraft, or other vehicle for which the State requires the operator or the owner of the vehicle, craft, or vessel to—(A) possess an operator's license; or (B) maintain insurance.[389]

This immunity does not apply to the charity itself but was created to encourage volunteers who otherwise might not provide their time to charity for fear of being sued.

388. Virginia recently reaffirmed the doctrine in *Ola v. YMCA of S. Hampton Rds., Inc.*, 621 S.E.2d 70 (Va. 2005).
389. P.L. 105-19, 4 (1997).

III. Spousal Immunity

326. Historically, spouses could not sue each other in tort. Modernly, most courts have completely abolished spousal immunity, though some states still retain spousal immunity for some torts. Strangers to the marriage can be affected by the interaction of spousal immunity, comparative fault, and joint and several liability. For example, in one case, two engaged people were visiting a theme park and one of them negligently injured the other on a ride. Before they sued the theme park they got married. The jury found the theme park 1% at fault and the two spouses at fault. But because of spousal immunity, the spouse that was primarily at fault for causing the injury could not be sued, and the theme park ended up absorbing nearly two-thirds of the judgment because of joint and several liability rules.[390]

IV. Parent-Child Immunity

327. In the past, parents were completely immune from lawsuits brought by their children. Over the course of the twentieth century, this broad immunity eroded. Today, some states have either abolished the immunity or limited it in some way. For those that retain the immunity, they generally hold parents immune for all acts related to the exercise of parental rights and the negligent provision of food, clothing, and housing.

V. Governmental Immunity

328. The federal and state governments are immune from suit unless they agree to be sued. This immunity derives from the government's sovereignty and the idea that the king cannot be sued by his subjects. In the twentieth century, both federal and state governments adopted legislation allowing some lawsuits to be brought against them, but only under statutorily approved conditions. For injuries that cannot be brought under governmental immunity waiver statutes, injured parties may petition the government directly and seek a private bill from Congress. At the federal level, this is done by having a member of the Senate or House of Representatives introduce a private bill granting a monetary award to the injured party and then seeking approval by both houses of Congress and the President.

§2. Firefighter's Rule (Professional Risk Takers)

329. Government workers that are required by their jobs to assume public safety perils may not sue those that they were hired to protect. The genesis of the rule was with firefighters, who attempted to sue landowners for the harm they suffered while fighting their fires. The rule has expanded and now includes other public safety

390. *Walt Disney World Co. v. Wood*, 489 So.2d 61 (Fla. Dist. Ct. App. 1986). The rule in this case was prospectively change by the Florida legislature.

workers that are required to place their lives in peril for the public good. In a sense, this rule is an application of the assumption of the risk doctrine since public safety workers are hired to assume certain risks. For example, a firefighter is injured by a falling roof while attempting to rescue someone in a burning building.

The firefighter assumed the risk that a roof might collapse. But, in situations where there was intentional misconduct, this rule does not act as a bar to recovery. In the burning building example, suppose that X intentionally started the fire as an act of arson. The injured fireman would not be barred from suing X.

§3. Federal Preemption of State Tort Law

I. Overview

330. Under the Constitution of the United States, the Federal Government enjoys broad powers in limiting State tort authority. What follows are some significant Federal limitations on the States, where traditional private law remedies have been eliminated or modified.

II. Public Readiness and Emergency Preparedness Act

331. The Public Readiness and Emergency Preparedness Act (PREP Act) was enacted in 2005 to provide immunity from civil liability for losses related to the administration or use of countermeasures during a current or future public emergency. Countermeasures are broadly understood to include some of the following: approved and unapproved drugs, biological products, or devices.[391] Except for willful actions (i.e., some action greater than negligence), "entities and individuals involved in the development, manufacture, testing, distribution, administration, and use of such countermeasures" are protected from civil tort liability.[392] Public emergencies are determined by the Secretary of the United States Department of Health and Human Services. Some current declarations include: smallpox, anthrax, and Zika virus. For those who suffer physical injury or death, the government has created the "Covered Countermeasures Process Fund," allowing for some compensation directly from the Federal Government.

III. Reporting Suspicious Activity Related to Air Travel

332. Air carriers and their employees are immune from civil liability when they report to Federal law-enforcement agents suspicious activities related to air piracy

391. Administration for Strategic Preparedness and Response. https://aspr.hhs.gov/legal/PREPact/Pages/PREP-Act-Question-and-Answers.aspx.

392. *Ibid.* https://aspr.hhs.gov/legal/PREPact/pages/default.aspx#:~:text=Public%20Readiness%20and%20Emergency%20Preparedness%20(PREP)%20Act,dependent%20on%2C%20other%20emergency%20declarations.

or plane safety.[393] For example, an airline employee might overhear a passenger talking about a "bomber," which he reports to a federal agent at the airport. The passenger is then escorted off the plane, where it is discovered he was only talking about bomber airplanes used by the air force. Normally, this passenger might be able to sue for false imprisonment, but under this act, the airline employee is immune from suit. Note that the immunity does not apply to knowingly or recklessly made false statements.

IV. Protection of Lawful Commerce in Arms Act

333. Since 2005, licensed manufacturers, retailers, and importers of firearms are generally immune from liability when guns are used in the commission of a crime.[394] Immunity does not extend to breach of contract, warranty, manufacturing defects, design defects, or negligent entrustment of a gun to someone likely to use the gun for criminal activity. Congress passed the legislation because they were concerned that third parties were trying to hold those in the gun trade liable for the independent acts of criminals.

V. Community Decency Act: Section 230

334. This statute provides interactive computer services—including social media platforms and internet service providers—broad immunity from liability for content posted by third-party users.[395] For example, a third party might post copyrighted material on a social media website or defamatory content on a website operated by an internet service provider. Normally, the two hosting sites might be civilly liable. But even when these sites have been informed that they have this information on their sites, they have no legal duty to remove the offending content.

393. 49 U.S.C.A §44941.
394. 15 U.S.C.A §§ 7901-7903.
395. 47 U.S.C.A. §230.

Part V. Causation

335. A person must be a cause of an injury to be held liable for a tort. In most situations, causation is not at issue and it is only in unusual circumstances that causation is litigated. For example, courts have no difficulty finding the driver of a speeding car that hits a pedestrian as the cause of the injury. There are two broad aspects to causation: actual cause and proximate cause. Actual cause determines whether a person was, in fact, in the chain of events that led to the injury. Proximate cause, also called legal cause, is a concept that limits recovery to those situations where there is a close connection between the actual cause and injury. Generally, causation is treated the same for intentional torts, negligence, and strict liability; however, proximate cause is stretched a bit more for intentional torts to capture conduct that is further removed from the harm.

§1. Actual Cause

336. The general rule is that "an act or omission is a cause-in-fact of an injury only if the injury could not have occurred without (or 'but for') that act or omission."[396] Although courts do not require a plaintiff to prove that a tortfeasor's "act or omission was the sole catalyst for his injuries, he must introduce evidence permitting the jury to conclude that the act or omission was a cause."[397] This burden of proof cannot be too speculative, and the plaintiff must prove more than "a mere possibility or a plausible explanation. Rather, a plaintiff establishes that the defendant's conduct was a cause-in-fact of his injuries only if he 'set[s] forth specific facts that would support a reasonable inference of a logical sequence of cause and effect.'"[398]

337. If there is a single cause connected to the injury then courts regularly use the "but for" test. This test asks, "But for the defendant's actions, would the tort have occurred?" One example includes: but for defendant intentionally hitting plaintiff in the nose, his nose would not have been broken. Single indivisible causes account for most tort actions, though there are situations where there are multiple indivisible causes of the injury. In one case a railroad's negligence caused a forest

396. *Craig ex rel Craig v. Oakwood Hosp.*, 684 N.W.2d 296 (Mich. 2004) (citing *Skinner v. Square D Co.*, 516 N.W.2d 475 (Mich. 1994)).
397. *Ibid.*
398. *Craig ex rel Craig v. Oakwood Hosp.*, 684 N.W.2d 296 (Mich. 2004) (citing *Skinner v. Square D Co.*, 516 N.W.2d 475 (Mich. 1994)).

fire, but simultaneously lightning caused another fire in the same forest. Both fires merged and eventually destroyed plaintiff's home.[399] In these situations, courts use the substantial factor test, where the courts ask if the defendant was a substantial factor in causing the harm. Substantial does not mean the primary cause, but rather the focus is on whether the defendant was in the causal link that contributed to the harm.

338. In some extremely rare situations, it is impossible or extremely difficult to determine the actual cause of an injury, though the tortfeasor must come from a readily identifiable small group of people. In *Summers v. Tice*, two hunters negligently shot in the direction of the plaintiff and a single shotgun pellet caused severe harm to the plaintiff's eye. Only one pellet, and thus only one hunter, could have caused the injury. The hunters argued that the plaintiff had the burden of establishing which of them was the cause of the injury—an impossibility under the circumstances. The court determined that the two hunters were acting in concert and shifted the burden of establishing causation to them, reasoning that they were in the best position to determine the actual tortfeasor.[400] This case led to the market share theory discussed in the next section.

339. Another difficult area involves manufacturers, often pharmaceutical companies, that all sell the same product, but the specific manufacturer that sold the defective product that injured the plaintiff cannot be identified. For example, Pharmaceutical Companies A, B, and C all sell Drug X. Over a period of a few years plaintiff purchases Drug X, a drug that is later determined to be dangerously defective. Some courts have used a market share theory to apportion liability based on a manufacturer's market share.[401] But this approach is difficult to apply equitably because there is no national court system that can adjudicate a truly national market share approach—one of the problems inherent with Federalism. For example, if Plaintiff sues Companies A, B, and C in a state, that state can apply a national market share approach or a state market share approach. If a state applies a state market place approach, it may not be sufficient as a number of plaintiffs may have moved from other states, where the apportionment formula is different. There will continue to be litigation in this area unless the federal government creates a national solution.

§2. Proximate or Legal Cause

I. Overview

340. Courts and lawyers are divided on what is included in the term proximate cause, also referred to as legal cause. Some courts treat proximate cause as a term

399. *Anderson v. Minneapolis, St. P. & S. St. M. Railroad Co.*, 179 N.W. 45 (Minn. 1920).
400. *Summers v. Tice*, 33 Cal.2d 80, 199 P.2d 1 (Cal. 1948).
401. *Sindell v. Abbott Laboratories*, 26 Cal. 3d 588 (Cal. 1980).

of art that includes both cause-in-fact and legal cause.[402] Others treat proximate cause as separate from cause-in-fact. In either case, the purpose of proximate cause is to determine when a defendant should be held liable for acts in which they were part of the causal link. In practice, proximate cause is used in exceptional cases to not hold someone liable even though they were a cause-in-fact of the plaintiff's injury. "The proximate cause issue, in spite of the terminology, is not about causation at all but about the appropriate scope of responsibility."[403] Judge Andrews noted:

> These two words have never been given an inclusive definition. What is a cause in a legal sense, still more what is a proximate cause, depend in each case upon many considerations, as does the existence of negligence itself. Any philosophical doctrine of causation does not help us. A boy throws a stone into a pond. The ripples spread. The water level rises. The history of that pond is altered to all eternity. It will be altered by other causes also. Yet it will be forever the resultant of all causes combined. Each one will have an influence. How great only omniscience can say. You may speak of a chain, or if you please, a net. An analogy is of little aid. Each cause brings about future events. Without each the future would not be the same. Each is proximate in the sense it is essential. But that is not what we mean by the word. Nor on the other hand do we mean sole cause. There is no such thing.[404]

341. A plaintiff is required to establish each element of their prima facie case, including proximate cause, and the jury determines whether the defendant was the proximate cause of the plaintiff's injury. In the vast majority of cases, proximate cause is not at issue because there is no reason to not hold the defendant liable for their actions. For example, a person that shoots a gun at another person is the cause-in-fact and proximate cause of the gun wound. In that case, cause-in-fact and proximate cause have merged. But suppose that a person legally shoots a gun at a bird, wounding the bird. The bird then flies for several miles, finally falling from the sky on someone's car, causing the person in the automobile to swerve and hit a tree. Proximate cause asks the question of whether the shooter should be held liable for causing the person in the automobile to crash. Obviously, the shooter is a cause-in-fact of the injury, but was it foreseeable at the time he shot the gun that someone several miles away would be injured? "What we do mean by the word 'proximate' is, that because of convenience, of public policy, of a rough sense of justice, the law arbitrarily declines to trace a series of events beyond a certain point. This is not logic. It is practical politics."[405]

---

402. *Craig ex rel Craig v. Oakwood Hosp.*, 684 N.W.2d 296 (Mich. 2004) (citing *Skinner v. Square D Co.*, 516 N.W.2d 475 (Mich. 1994)).

403. Dan B. Dobbs, *The Law of Torts* §180, 443 (Thompson-West 2000).

404. *Palsgraf v. Long Island Railroad Co.*, 162 N.E. 99 (N.Y. 1928), *reh'g denied*, 164 N.E. 564 (N.Y. 1928) (Andrews, dissent).

405. *Ibid.*

II. Proximate Cause Test: Foreseeability Standard

342. The modern approach to proximate cause focuses on reasonable foreseeability—a defendant is liable for the injuries caused by their conduct if they reasonably should have foreseen the consequences of their actions. In most tort cases foreseeability is not at issue with courts instructing juries to determine if the plaintiff's injury was the reasonable, ordinary, natural, or probable consequence of the defendant's action. Therefore, it is only in cases of unforeseeability that proximate cause needs to be analyzed in any meaningful way. Stated in the negative, a defendant is not the proximate cause of an injury when there is (1) an unforeseeable type of injury; (2) an unforeseeable plaintiff; or (3) an unforeseeable intervening event.

343. The unforeseeable type of injury or harm is the most common proximate cause issue. The Restatement (Third) of Torts recasts the test as one dealing with the type of risk (i.e., a risk standard) created by the defendant, but otherwise still uses foreseeability as a guide.[406] Some courts label proximate cause as "remote harm" to deal with those that are connected to the injury but that no reasonable person would find them liable for the injury. For example, the mother of a mass murderer is clearly part of the chain of events that led to the murders, in the sense that "but for" giving birth to the murderer, the murders could never have occurred. Though the mother is an actual cause of the murders, her connection to the harm is too remote to hold her liable for her son's actions. More likely cases of an unforeseeable type of harm are illustrated in the following two examples:

> Richard, a hunter, finishes his day in the field and stops at a friend's house while walking home. His friend's nine-year-old daughter, Kim, greets Richard, who hands his loaded shotgun to her as he enters the house. Kim drops the shotgun, which lands on her toe, breaking it. Although Richard was negligent for giving Kim his shotgun, the risk that made Richard negligent was that Kim might shoot someone with the gun, not that she would drop it and hurt herself (the gun was neither especially heavy nor unwieldy). Kim's broken toe is outside the scope of Richard's liability, even though Richard's tortious conduct was a factual cause of Kim's harm.[407]
>
> James provided a company-owned automobile to Henry for personal and business use, despite his poor driving record. While on vacation, Henry went out with Michelle and, at the end of the evening, asked her to drive home. While Michelle was driving, she negligently ran into Vivian, a pedestrian. Vivian introduces no evidence that Henry had a propensity to lend his car to other poor drivers. Vivian's harm is outside the scope of liability of any negligence by James in entrusting the automobile to Henry, as a matter of law. (Whether James is liable as the owner of the automobile is a different matter not addressed by this Illustration.)[408]

---

406. Restatement (Third) of Torts: Liab. Physical Harm §29 (2005).
407. *Ibid.* (Illust. 3).
408. *Ibid.* (Illust. 5).

344. In some cases, the type of harm was foreseeable but the manner in which the harm occurred was unforeseeable. In one case an employee was working near a furnace, using gasoline to clean equipment. A rat ran into the furnace, caught on fire, ran near the gasoline, and caused an explosion. The employer was the proximate cause of the explosion because an explosion was a reasonably foreseeable type of harm even though the manner in which the explosion occurred was extremely unusual.[409] Thus, a defendant remains liable for reasonably foreseeable harm even though the exact manner in which the harm occurred was unforeseeable. The rationale is that once a defendant engages in tortious conduct they should not be relieved of liability when the predictable risk actually occurs, regardless if it occurs in a freakish manner.

345. A defendant will not be relieved of liability under proximate cause when there is an unforeseeable extent of injury. A common application of this rule involves what is traditionally called the "thin skull" or "eggshell" plaintiff—a plaintiff that suffers greater harm than most people due to a preexisting medical or mental condition. For example:

> Jennifer was driving her automobile, manufactured by the Edison Motor Co., on an Interstate highway when the voltage regulator in the car failed due to negligent installation. The failure caused the battery fluid to boil, which produced toxic fumes that reached the interior of the car. Jennifer suffered chronic vocal-cord dysfunction as a result. Jennifer was a popular vocal performer who earned several million dollars each year. All of Jennifer's lost earnings due to her vocal-cord injury are within the scope of Edison's liability for its negligence, as a matter of law.[410]

346. There are cases where the plaintiff claims that they themselves were unforeseeable in relation to the defendant. The problem of the unforeseeable plaintiff begins not with foreseeability, but rather with the question of whether this is a duty issue or proximate cause issue. A defendant may only recover from those plaintiffs that owe a duty of care to him, and if no duty is owed then there is no recovery. In the context of a plaintiff that owes no duty to a particular defendant, it is understood that the plaintiff is necessarily unforeseeable. In the first part of the twentieth century, courts tended to deal with the unforeseeable plaintiff under the duty element, thereby deciding this issue as a matter of law. Courts today still determine whether a plaintiff owes the defendant a duty of care, but most courts would leave this issue to the jury under the proximate cause element, except in cases where there is no reasonable basis for claiming the plaintiff owed the defendant any duty. For example, a person is injured while swimming in the ocean and they decide to sue a large department store because the store has large cash reserves. The store will ask and the court will grant the store's motion to dismiss the action because there is no reasonable basis for holding the store liable as the store did not owe the plaintiff a duty

409. *United Novelty Co. v. Daniels*, 42 So.2d 395 (Miss. 1949).
410. Restatement (Third) of Torts: Liab. Physical Harm §31 (2005) (Illust. 3).

of care under these circumstances. But, if the injury was related to defective swimwear, then the judge should allow the jury to decide whether the plaintiff was foreseeable under proximate cause.

347. Finally, there is the unforeseeable intervening event, where an independent act by another or an act of nature joins with the defendant's conduct and thereby breaks the link to the defendant. The rationale for not holding the defendant liable is that the risk the defendant created by his tortious conduct becomes radically different when combined with the unforeseeable intervening event. While an act of nature, such as lightning, might be an unforeseeable intervening event, it only becomes so if the risk of harm is different from what was reasonably foreseeable at the time of the defendant's tortious conduct. A common unforeseeable intervening event often includes criminal conduct. The following two examples deal with similar facts but two different results:

> David, a private security guard, personally purchased a walkie-talkie designed for children as a toy and manufactured by the Hohe Toy Co. David took one of the receivers to work and left the other with his brother, Gary. One night, while inspecting an empty warehouse whose door was left open, David was accosted by several thieves. David attempted to contact Gary to call for help, but a defective switch in the walkie-talkie prevented David from contacting Gary. The thieves attacked and injured David who sues Hohe for the harm he suffered in the attack. Despite the defect in Hohe's walkie-talkie, Hohe is not liable for David's harm as a matter of law, because the attack by the thieves produced harm that was not among the risks that one might consider in determining that, at the time of manufacture, the walkie-talkie was defective.[411]

Same facts as [above], except that the walkie-talkie is manufactured by Stand Tall, Inc., a company that specializes in security equipment for law-enforcement personnel, and the walkie-talkie was designed and marketed for use by law-enforcement officials. Stand Tall's liability for selling a defective walkie-talkie includes the harm suffered by David in the attack by the thieves, as a matter of law.[412]

§3. Multiple Tortfeasors

348. Recognized in the United States since the late 1700s, joint and several liability subjects each tortfeasor involved in plaintiff's injuries to liability. Consequently, a plaintiff may seek and obtain a judgment against one or all of the responsible parties. Under the theory of joint and several liability, however, a plaintiff may only receive his total damages, not more, regardless of how many defendants are involved. Although some jurisdictions have statutory limitations for cases involving

411. Restatement (Third) of Torts: Liab. Physical Harm §34 (2005) (Illust. 6).
412. Restatement (Third) of Torts: Liab. Physical Harm §34 (2005) (Illust. 7).

more than one tortfeasor, the primary rules regarding apportionment of responsibility among multiple defendants can be categorized as follows:

1. actions in concert;
2. an indivisible injury;
3. vicarious liability; and
4. joint and several liability.

349. When two or more parties "act in concert or unity of action," the general rule is that each party is jointly and severally liable to the plaintiff for all of his harm.[413] This principle applies to defendants who "intentionally unite" in the tortious act, as well as those "who are present and assist or participate therein," so that the resultant harm stems from these parties' joint venture.[414] The reasoning behind assessing joint and several liability, rather than apportionment, in cases where parties act in concert, is set forth in the Restatement and generally adopted by the courts as follows:

> [P]ersons are acting in concert if (1) a tortious act is performed in concert or pursuant to a common design, (2) an act known to be tortious is encouraged or substantially assisted, or (3) substantial assistance is rendered to accomplish a tortious result if such assistance itself constitutes a breach of duty. In our view, each of these scenarios depicts a single and indivisible course of tortious conduct for which each is an equal participant and equally liable. The conduct of one actor cannot be compared to the conduct of another for purposes of apportioning liability because each agreed to cooperate in the tortious conduct or tortious result and each is liable for the entirety of the damages as if there were but one actor.[415]

350. In addition to united action, it is possible that independent action that causes a single harm may create liability for the joint tortfeasors:

> Joint and several liability arises in tort claims based on the conduct of the tortfeasors and the nature of the injury. "If the independent tortious conduct of two or more persons is a legal cause of an indivisible injury, each person is jointly and severally liable for the recoverable damages caused by the tortious conduct."[416]

351. The concepts of vicarious liability and joint and several liability are:

---

413. *Bergman by Harre v. Anderson*, 411 N.W.2d 336, 338 (Neb. 1987).
414. *Ibid.*
415. *Woods v. Cole*, 675 N.E.2d 132, 133 (Ill. App. Ct. 1996) (citing Restatement (Second) of Torts §876 (1979)).
416. *CTTI Priesmeyer, Inc. v. K & O Ltd. Partnership*, 164 S.W.3d 675 (Tex. App. 2005) (quoting Restatement (Third) of Torts: Apportionment of Liability §A18 (2000)).

> not interchangeable. In Murray v. Helfrich, 146 Or. 602, 605-06, 30 P.2d 1053 (1934), the court described joint and several liability as follows: "[W]here the negligence of two or more persons concur in producing a single, indivisible injury, then such persons are jointly and severally liable, although there was no common duty, common design or concerted action." ... Vicarious liability is different. In Doe v. Oregon Conference of Seventh-Day Adventists, 199 Or. App. 319, 328, 111 P.3d 791 (2005), we noted: "The theory of vicarious liability imposes liability on one person for the acts of another. The term encompasses a variety of situations: coconspirators, partners, and joint venturers can all be vicariously liable for each other's torts or crimes. When the 'person' upon which liability ultimately rests is a fictive person, that is, a corporation, the only kind of liability that can conceivably exist is vicarious[.]" ... Thus, a defendant that is vicariously liable for the actions of another person might be held jointly and severally liable (assuming that the other person was also a defendant in the case, which certainly is not necessary in order to establish vicarious liability). But the obverse is not true: One may not assume from the fact that liability of two defendants in a case is joint and several that each is responsible for the entire amount based on a theory of vicarious liability.[417]

As the Kansas Supreme Court explained:

> The concept of joint and several liability between joint tortfeasors which previously existed in this state no longer applies in comparative negligence actions. The individual liability of each defendant for payment of damages is to be based on proportionate fault, and contribution among joint judgment debtors is no longer needed in such cases because separate individual judgments are to be rendered .... In actions where comparative negligence is in issue the court deals in percentages of causal responsibility, and distinctions between primary, secondary, active and passive negligence lose their previous identities. The nature of misconduct in such cases is to be expressed on the basis of degrees of comparative fault or causation, and the "all or nothing" concepts are swept aside. Courts have always taken the position that compromise and settlement of disputes between parties should be favored in the law in the absence of fraud or bad faith. There is no reason in a comparative liability jurisdiction to hold a defendant, the proposed indemnitor, liable for damages in disproportion to his causal fault. Similarly, there is no reason to deny another defendant, the proposed indemnitee, a right of liability reduction when his fault, although minimal in terms of causal involvement, may nevertheless be characterized as "active." We conclude that now is the proper time under the facts of this case to adopt a form of comparative implied indemnity between joint tortfeasors. When, as here, a settlement for plaintiffs' entire injuries or damages has been made by one tortfeasor during the pendency of a comparative negligence action and a release of all liability has been given by plaintiffs

---

417. *American Federation of Teachers-Oregon, AFT, AFL-CIO v. Oregon Taxpayers United PAC*, 149 P.3d 159, 163 (Or. Ct. App. 2006).

to all who may have contributed to said damages, apportionment of responsibility can then be pursued in the action among the tortfeasors. In any action where apportionment of responsibility is sought by a settling tortfeasor, he or she will be required to establish the reasonableness of the amount of the settlement and that he or she had an actual legal liability for the injuries and damage which he or she should not be expected to successfully resist.[418]

418. *Kennedy v. City of Sawyer*, 228 Kan. 439, 618 P.2d 788 (Kan., 1980).

Part VI. Remedies

Chapter 1. General Principles

352. The primary goal behind tort law is to make the injured person whole and in some cases to punish bad conduct. Compensatory damages, or actual damages, are those amounts that indemnify the injured party for all of their losses. The injured party should be placed back into the position they were in before the injury, without any profit resulting from the injury. Examples of actual damages include medical bills, pain and suffering, property replacement, and lost wages. In rare cases, non-compensatory damages (i.e., punitive damages) are awarded to punish exceptionally bad conduct. The purpose behind non-compensatory damages is to punish the conduct of the wrongdoer and not to compensate the injured party, though the injured party is compensated in the sense that in most jurisdictions they get to keep the award. For intentional torts where a plaintiff establishes a tort but does not prove actual harm, nominal damages are generally available. Finally, in some cases, equitable remedies, such as restitution and the injunction, may be available.

353. From a practice perspective, it is best to plead the specific damages that the plaintiff is requesting in litigation (e.g., medical cost, lost profits, pain and suffering, etc.). Courts, practitioners, and scholars are divided on the exact meaning of many remedy terms, and failing to plead a specific harm can lead to that harm being denied. Further complicating the terminology problem is that damage terms can change meaning between tort law and contract law because commercial contracts tend to be governed by statute, while tort law tends to be governed by the common law. With some tort claims deriving from contract (i.e., warranty in products liability), the same cause of action could have damages defined in two different ways.

Chapter 2. Kinds of Damages

§1. Individual and Collective Damage

354. The vast majority of tort damages involve individual damages rather than collective damages. Even in cases where a wrongdoer injured thousands of people, the courts will try to provide an individualized damage award, and if that is impracticable then place those harmed into various classes of similarly situated people. For example, if a pharmaceutical company sells a dangerously defective product that results in thousands of people being injured, plaintiffs will likely bring a class action lawsuit and the courts will attempt to sort victims into various classes. Those with kidney failure into one class, those with heart valve problems in another, and so on. But this process is to help with administration of claims and not because it is viewed as superior to individual damage awards.

355. One area where collective damages are routinely awarded involves civil rights violations. For example, it was common in the 1960s for a school district to be sued for discriminating against those of the African race. The remedy was collective in nature because it applied to all those of African descent living in the district. A remedy might require a certain percentage of minority students to attend an all-white school.

§2. Direct and Indirect

356. Direct damages have a direct causal connection with the injury and indirect damages are intermediate consequences of the injury. The North Carolina Supreme Court explained:

> [A] tortfeasor "is responsible for all damages directly caused by his misconduct, and for all indirect or consequential damages which are the natural and probable effect of the wrong, under the facts as they exist at the time the same is committed and which can be ascertained with a reasonable degree of certainty."[419]

While most jurisdictions call indirect damages "consequential damages," others refer to them as "special damages."

357. All damages must be proved and direct damages are easier to establish (i.e., a medical bill for a broken leg after an automobile accident). Consequential damages cannot be speculative; therefore, courts require the plaintiff to establish consequential damages with evidence of the harm. But this is nothing more than requiring the plaintiff to prove that the defendant is the proximate cause of the

419. *Watts v. North Carolina Dep't of Env't and Natural Res.*, 641 S.E.2d 811 (N.C. Ct. App. 2007) (citing *Binder v. General Motors Acceptance Corp.*, 23 S.E.2d 894, 895 (N.C. 1943)) (quoting *Conrad v. Shuford*, 94 S.E. 424, 425 (N.C. 1917)).

injury. Injuries that are farther removed from the defendant are less likely to be proven. For example, a plaintiff might have been on his way to audition for an acting position, but because of the defendant's negligence, he missed his audition. It is unlikely that the plaintiff will recover future lost wages for the high-paying job based on his testimony that he might have received the position. Speculative and uncertain damages are not recoverable.

§3. Pecuniary and Nonpecuniary Losses

358. Pecuniary damages are those, like medical bills or lost wages, that can be measured by money, and nonpecuniary damages are those, like pain and suffering, that cannot be measured by money. Both types are available and must be proven to the fact finder. The greatest controversies exist around nonpecuniary damages, with over half of the states with statutory caps on them. Statutory caps have reduced the number of lawsuits and reduced the amount of pecuniary damages available to a victim. Because many injured cannot afford to hire a lawyer, personal injury lawyers usually accept clients on a contingency fee basis. Until recently the attorney could hope to get an award with a significant pain and suffering component, using that component for legal fees and the rest of the award for pecuniary damages. This is important because in the United States, each side pays for its own legal fees and the loser does not pay for the legal fees of the winner. Thus, with recent statutory limitations on pain and suffering damages, there is now less for the victim to cover his pecuniary damages after paying legal fees.

§4. Pure Economic Loss

359. Pure economic loss must generally be recovered under contract law and not tort law. For a discussion on the interaction between negligence and contract law, *see* the discussion in Part I, Chapter 3.

§5. Actual and Future Damage (Lost Profits)

360. Two broad categories of damages are actual damages and special damages; however, because damages vary depending on the cause of action, courts generally do not use broad terms to measure damages. Actual damages, also called compensatory damages or general damages, provide monetary awards for proven harm and are meant to reimburse the losses suffered by the plaintiff. But only if the actual damages are proximately, necessarily, or naturally related to the tortious conduct. Actual damages do not include special or punitive damages.

361. Special damages, also called consequential damages, are available for harm indirectly related to the tort—"damages … that ensue, not necessarily or ordinarily, but because of special circumstances."[420] Special damages generally include claims for lost profits. The level of proof is higher than with compensatory damages, generally requiring a plaintiff to establish more than a realized loss—the loss must be recognized or highly likely to occur. For example, a plaintiff may sue someone claiming that they purchased some stock because of that person's fraudulent misrepresentation, but until the stock is sold the loss has only been realized and not yet recognized.

In practice, specific damages should be pleaded in detail rather than using the general terms indicated in this section because courts do not employ common definitions from state to state, and possibly even from court to court in the same state. For example, one court explained that "the classification of compensatory damages as either general or special damages is specific to the cause of action being discussed."[421] While the court may be correct in stating that the damage classification will change based on the cause of action, it is clear that the court views general damages and special damages as a category under compensatory damages. Other courts view compensatory damages as different from special damages. Likewise, some courts view actual damages as those that can be determined with exact precision and therefore are synonymous with pecuniary damages, while other courts view actual damages as encompassing both pecuniary and nonpecuniary harm. Finally, special damages are also subject to different treatment, with one court treating them as a type of punitive damages.[422] Again, caution should be used when discussing actual and special damages because they are subject to multiple and inconsistent interpretations.

§6. Other Costs

362. Under what is called the American Rule, all litigants are responsible to pay their own court costs and legal fees. In some circumstances, a statute, such as civil rights cases or cases involving securities violations, or a contractual obligation may allow a plaintiff to recover reasonable attorney fees from the defendant. Also, attorney fees may be granted when one party engages in wrongful conduct in bringing the litigation or wrongful conduct during the course of the litigation.

§7. Mitigation of Damages

363. Every injured person has a duty to mitigate their damages and failure to do so may extinguish any claims they may have against the wrongdoer from the moment that they failed to act reasonably. For example, an injured person taken to

420. *Ruggles v. Buffalo Foundry & Mach. Co.*, 27 F.2d 234 (6th Cir. 1928).
421. *Musa v. Jefferson County Bank*, 620 N.W.2d 797 (Wis. 2001).
422. *Sias v. General Motors Corp.*, 127 N.W.2d 357, 362 (Mich. 1964).

a hospital after an accident may be told by a physician that they need to take antibiotics for two weeks. The injured person fails to act reasonably and fails to take their medicine, resulting in an infection that requires the removal of their leg—the leg could have been saved if the antibiotics had been taken. The wrongdoer is not liable for the lost leg.

364. The doctrine is sometimes referred to as the avoidable consequences doctrine and is separate from any comparative fault calculation because there are two distinct events: the initial injury and the subsequent failure to mitigate damages. A wrongdoer is only liable for all reasonably foreseeable harm, and failing to mitigate damages is not foreseeable. This doctrine is extremely important in modified comparative fault jurisdictions and in contributory fault jurisdictions as it helps to separate the plaintiff's unreasonable conduct (i.e., failure to mitigate damages) from the initial injury. Without this doctrine a jury might view all of the injuries together, resulting in a plaintiff not recovering for the initial injuries.

§8. Nominal Damages

365. In some instances, a plaintiff may prove a technical violation of a tort or fail to provide evidence on the exact amount of damages, which will result in the award of nominal damages. "Nominal damages are allowed, not as an equivalent for the wrong … and are not the same as damages small in amount."[423] Older cases awarded six cents, while most modern courts will award USD 1 or USD 3. It should be noted that there is no connection between the awarded amount and the tort—the amount is awarded for the sole purpose of perfecting the tort.

366. Nominal damages are always available for intentional torts. For example, a person may spit on the boots of another, causing no damage; however, this would constitute a battery because intentionally spitting on another is offensive to a reasonable person. The owner of the boot would be entitled to nominal damages, likely USD 1. Negligence cases require the plaintiff to prove damages. In some rare cases, the plaintiff proves actual harm but then fails to prove the exact amount, and thus nominal damages may be awarded. For example, the plaintiff proves that the defendant negligently hit their car while intoxicated but then fails to provide any evidence as to the amount of the damage. The court should award nominal damages under those facts.

367. Finally, nominal damages may be important in getting punitive damages. Many states do not allow punitive damages unless some damage can be established. Thus, it may be critical to establish nominal damages—USD 1—to get to a much larger punitive damage award.

423. *Cowan v. Flannery*, 461 N.W.2d 155, 159 (Iowa 1990).

Chapter 3. Assessment and Compensation of Damages

§1. Objective Versus Subjective

368. The terms *objective* and *subjective* are rarely used to describe the assessment of tort damages in the United States. Objective damages include those costs that are not speculative, but rather reasonable in the mind of the trier of fact. Objective items include medical costs, lost wages, nursing care, or prescription drugs. Subjective damages are those costs that are more speculative in nature, such as pain and suffering, loss of consortium, and other emotional harm.

§2. Concrete Versus Abstract

369. The terms *concrete* and *abstract* are generally not used in the United States to discuss damage assessment and compensation. *See* the discussion above under §1 "Objective Versus Subjective" for information concerning this topic.

§3. Methods of Assessing Damages

370. There is no single rule for assessing tort damages as every damage award should be sufficient to reasonably compensate a victim for harm done—the standard is justice and fairness. While the trier of fact has a great deal of discretion in the amount they award, judges are required to exercise their discretion in lowering exceptionally large awards that are unreasonable. In some physical injury cases, the trier of fact may take into account the plaintiff's health, sex, occupation, or age in determining the appropriate damage award. For example, if a person is permanently disabled or dies because of the defendant's tortious conduct, then those factors are relevant in determining lost wages and life expectancy using actuarial tables. As the Supreme Court of the United States explained:

> it has never been held that the rules to be derived from such tables or computations must be the absolute guides of the judgment and the conscience of the jury. On the contrary, in the important and much considered case of Phillips v. London & S. W. Ry … the judges strongly approved the usual practice of instructing the jury in general terms to award a fair and reasonable compensation, taking into consideration what the plaintiff's income would probably have been, how long it would have lasted, and all the contingencies to which it was liable; and as strongly deprecated undertaking to bind them by precise mathematical rules in deciding a question involving so many contingencies incapable of exact estimate or proof.[424]

---

424. *Vicksburg & M.R. Co. v. Putnam*, 118 U.S. 545, 554 (1886).

For damage to property, the goal is to compensate for the actual loss, without enriching the plaintiff. If a plaintiff has been deprived of his property, then the proper method for determining the amount of damages is the fair rental value of the property during the time of the deprivation. When property is completely destroyed, the method used is the property's fair market value right before the destruction.

§4. Equitable Limitation of Damages

371. Courts have the discretion to reduce excessive damage awards, generally if requested by the losing party. If a court grants remittitur, the plaintiff either is allowed a new trial or a judicially determined amount that is lower than the amount awarded by the jury. Many states have statutorily capped some awards, specifically pain and suffering, and punitive damages. Juries in most states are not informed about the caps and if they award amounts in excess of the caps then the judge reduces the award to the statutorily approved amount. If there are multiple defendants it is possible that the statute will be interpreted to allow the maximum amount for each defendant over a single cap for the entire injury.

§5. Methods of Payment

372. The most common method of payment is the lump-sum payment for all damages and that amount is determined at the time of trial, even when some portion of the lump-sum payment is for damages that will occur in the future (e.g., future medical expenses or future lost wages). Though parties are free to suggest alternate payment methods to the court, courts are reluctant to consider them because it means additional oversight by the court. In the case of a plaintiff that wants to receive an annuity, it is quite likely that the court will have the tortfeasor deposit the payment with an annuity provider rather than receiving periodic payments directly from the defendant. Because of the lump-sum preference, some judgments will be over-inclusive and others under-inclusive. Over-inclusive when, in the example of future wages, the injured party dies years before the actuarial tables indicated death, and likewise under-inclusive when the injured party lives many years beyond their life expectancy. Mechanically, payment in a personal injury suit will often be made to the plaintiff's attorney to ensure that funds are available to cover legal fees.

§6. Multiple Tortfeasors

I. Joint and Several Liability

373. Joint and several liability is the traditional common-law rule, altered significantly today, that allows a plaintiff to decide which defendant to hold liable when there is more than one tortfeasor. The rationale behind the rule is to ensure that a plaintiff has the opportunity to recover for their harm from at least one defendant, even when one tortfeasor is insolvent, dead, or personal jurisdiction is not available. The common-law rule requires all joint tortfeasors to be responsible for their pro rata portion of the damage award, though if for some reason one or more of the joint tortfeasors does not or cannot pay for the damages then the plaintiff can seek damages from any of the tortfeasors that are available to pay the claim. In the event that the damages are not paid on a pro rata basis because of the joint and several liability rule, then the defendants that paid a higher portion of the damages may sue the nonpaying tortfeasors for contribution or indemnity. For example, X, Y, and Z are joint tortfeasors in a lawsuit brought by P. P chooses to sue Y because P despises Y more than the others, even though X, Y, and Z each have sufficient funds to cover the damages they inflicted on P. Y will be required to pay 100% of the damages under joint and several liability, though Y can bring X and Z in as codefendants to avoid a separate contribution action at a later time. Because of the perceived inequity among joint tortfeasors, most states have either abolished or altered joint and several liability.

II. Contribution and Indemnification

374. Joint tortfeasors that pay all or a portion of the plaintiff's damages are entitled to contribution from nonpaying tortfeasors if the paying tortfeasor paid more than their share of the liability. However, contribution is generally not allowed to intentional tortfeasors. For example:

> A sues B, C, and D for an indivisible injury sustained in an automobile accident. A obtains a judgment against B, C, and D whereby they are jointly and severally liable to A for USD 100,000. The fact finder assigns 50% responsibility to B, 30% responsibility to C, and 20% responsibility to D. B pays A the entire judgment. Subject to the other requirements of this Section, B may recover contribution from C or D for a total of USD 50,000 (USD 100,000 × 0.50), because B's satisfaction of the judgment extinguished C's and D's liability to A.[425]

375. One of the requirements for contribution is that the joint tortfeasors shared a common liability. A situation where there is no common liability is when an employer and a third party are joint tortfeasors. Workers' compensation immunizes an employer when the employee suffers a work-related injury, but workers' compensation does not immunize a third-party tortfeasor. Therefore, that third-party tortfeasor does not have a common liability with the injured person's employer and may not seek contribution from that employer. For example, an employer negligently maintains the brakes in a company-owned vehicle, which is a causal factor in an accident with a third person that was speeding. In a lawsuit by the employee against the third person that was speeding, that third person will not be able to recover from injured person's negligent employer for contribution.

425. Restatement (Third) of Torts: Apportionment Liab. §23 (2000) (Illust. 1).

376. Indemnity is narrower than joint and several liability and is available when one defendant is sued for damages but another party is responsible for the damages. The Restatement on Apportionment of Liability explains:

a. When two or more persons are or may be liable for the same harm and one of them discharges the liability of another in whole or in part by settlement or discharge of judgment, the person discharging the liability is entitled to recover indemnity in the amount paid to the plaintiff, plus reasonable legal expenses, if:
   1. the indemnitor has agreed by contract to indemnify the indemnitee; or
   2. the indemnitee:
      – was not liable except vicariously for the tort of the indemnitor; or
      – was not liable except as a seller of a product supplied to the indemnitee by the indemnitor and the indemnitee was not independently culpable.
b. A person who is otherwise entitled to recover indemnity pursuant to contract may do so even if the party against whom indemnity is sought would not be liable to the plaintiff.[426]

One situation where indemnity is appropriate is when an employer, who has been sued by a plaintiff under vicarious liability for their employee's on-the-job negligence, sues their negligent employee for 100% of the damages they paid to the plaintiff. Also, in a strict products liability action, any commercial seller may have to pay the claim, and that party has a right to indemnity from the manufacturer. Finally, a contract may contain an indemnity clause and shift the liability to another, even one who is not responsible for the tort.

III. Allocations of Liability among Joint Tortfeasors

377. Joint and several liability is a good way to help plaintiffs recover for their injuries, but it does not address the problem of the slightly negligent joint tortfeasor that is required to pay the entire tort claim. Comparative fault is a method to allow juries to allocate fault between the injured person and all joint tortfeasors. In one case a couple were racing go-carts at a theme park when the male purposely bumped into the female, causing her severe back injuries. Before filing suit against the theme park they were married, which meant that spousal immunity protected the husband from suit. At trial, the jury determined that the wife was 14% at fault, the husband 85% at fault, and the theme park 1% at fault. Because of joint and several liability, and the husband's immunity from suit, the theme park was required to cover 86% of the damages to the plaintiff's wife.[427]

378. Most states have abolished or significantly altered joint and several liability. One group of states has abolished it with some exceptions. A second group of states that abolished it will recalculate the joint tortfeasors' comparative fault if one or more tortfeasors are unable to pay. A third group of states has abolished it for

426. Restatement (Third) of Torts: Apportionment Liab. §22 (2000).
427. *Walt Disney World Co. v. Wood*, 515 So.2d 198 (Fla. 1987).

tortfeasors below a statutorily defined comparative fault percentage. And the fourth group of states has retained joint and several liability for economic damages but abolished it for noneconomic damages.

IV. Settlement of Claims

379. Settlement of a claim involving multiple tortfeasors needs to be handled carefully. At common law, settling with one joint tortfeasor and releasing him from suit resulted in releasing all the other tortfeasors as well because the plaintiff had given up the cause of action—this view is disfavored today though may exist in a few states. Attorneys then came up with settlements that created a covenant by the plaintiff not to sue the settling party. But because the plaintiff could sue the remaining tortfeasors, the remaining tortfeasors could sue the settling tortfeasor for contribution if a jury awarded a larger than expected amount. The answer to this problem is for the plaintiff to guarantee in the settlement agreement that they will indemnify the settling tortfeasor for any amount above the agreed settlement amount. As one court noted:

> The concept of joint and several liability between joint tortfeasors which previously existed in this state no longer applies in comparative negligence actions. The individual liability of each defendant for payment of damages is to be based on proportionate fault, and contribution among joint judgment debtors is no longer needed in such cases because separate individual judgments are to be rendered .... In actions where comparative negligence is in issue the court deals in percentages of causal responsibility, and distinctions between primary, secondary, active and passive negligence lose their previous identities. The nature of misconduct in such cases is to be expressed on the basis of degrees of comparative fault or causation, and the "all or nothing" concepts are swept aside. Courts have always taken the position that compromise and settlement of disputes between parties should be favored in the law in the absence of fraud or bad faith. There is no reason in a comparative liability jurisdiction to hold a defendant, the proposed indemnitor, liable for damages in disproportion to his causal fault. Similarly, there is no reason to deny another defendant, the proposed indemnitee, a right of liability reduction when his fault, although minimal in terms of causal involvement, may nevertheless be characterized as "active." We conclude that now is the proper time under the facts of this case to adopt a form of comparative implied indemnity between joint tortfeasors. When, as here, a settlement for plaintiffs' entire injuries or damages has been made by one tortfeasor during the pendency of a comparative negligence action and a release of all liability has been given by plaintiffs to all who may have contributed to said damages, apportionment of responsibility can then be pursued in the action among the tortfeasors. In any action where apportionment of responsibility is sought by a settling tortfeasor, he or

she will be required to establish the reasonableness of the amount of the settlement and that he or she had an actual legal liability for the injuries and damage which he or she should not be expected to successfully resist.[428]

428. *Teepak, Inc. v. Learned*, 699 P.2d 35, 41–42 (Kan. 1985).

Chapter 4. Personal Injury and Death

§1. Pecuniary Losses

380. Pecuniary damages are available to a plaintiff, generally without any limitation, and include expenses directly related to the injury, and lost wages. Reasonable medical expenses necessary to treat the patient are available and may include care by doctors, nurses, hospitals, nursing homes, drugs, and medical devices (e.g., wheelchairs or prosthetic limbs). Other expenses related to the injury are recoverable, such as transportation and housekeeping expenses for quadriplegia, or the expenses related to rearing a disabled child to maturity for the tort of wrongful birth. Future medical expenses are also recoverable and include future surgery, medical care, medical monitoring, or any other reasonably provable expense. Finally, costs are recoverable for property that was damaged by the tortfeasor.

381. Compensatory damage awards in personal injury cases where there was some physical harm are not subject to federal income tax. With marginal tax rates close to 40%, this is a significant benefit to tort victims. This exclusion from gross income is broad and includes medical bills, pain and suffering, past lost wages, and future lost wages. Punitive damages are not excluded from gross income and any claims involving pure emotional harm are also not excluded.

§2. Nonpecuniary Losses

382. Pain and suffering awards are allowed once personal injury is established. The jury may infer the amount of emotional harm based on the nature of the injury and available testimony. In addition to current pain and suffering, the jury may award future pain and suffering. The manifestation of the negative emotional state may take different forms, such as mental pain related to disfigurement, the loss of pleasure, constant pain, or fear of a shortened life. One requirement is that the injured person be conscious of the pain and suffering. For example, in the situation where a person goes into a coma at the time of the accident, there is no consciousness, and therefore pain and suffering are disallowed. But if it can be proven that there was even a short period of consciousness, then the fact finder may award pain and suffering.

383. One type of emotional harm occurs when someone is currently fearful for possible future harm. For example, this can occur when a person is exposed to a toxic substance, which is known to cause cancer for some people in twenty years. If there is a current tort connected to the potential future harm then there is little difficulty in allowing a future pain and suffering award. The complicated case involves a current fear of potential harm in the future, especially when the potential harm is remote. For example, a plaintiff is exposed to a known carcinogen and there is a 30% chance that they will develop cancer in forty years. The current fear is real and there is no recourse for the plaintiff in forty years if they develop cancer because of the statute of limitations. Courts generally deal with these cases using proximate cause, limiting recovery in remote cases and allowing recovery when future harm is reasonably likely to occur.

384. One approach to helping the fact finder with establishing a pain and suffering award, especially when there is severe injury, is the "day-in-the-life" video. Generally, a camera crew arrives at the plaintiff's home early in the morning and shows the plaintiff wake up and follows them through the day, demonstrating the difficulty of living with a severe injury. The jury will not see the entire film but only those parts edited by the plaintiff, with the film likely including staged events to help dramatize the film.

385. Because of the concern with perceived high pain and suffering awards, many states have statutorily limited pain and suffering awards. The most common approach is by placing a cap on the award in the form of a maximum amount that may be awarded. Some states limit the caps to certain types of cases, such as medical malpractice. Juries are generally not informed of the cap and if they award an amount higher than the cap, that pain and suffering amount is lowered to the statutory cap.

§3. Wrongful Death and Survival Statutes

386. At common law, death extinguished all tort claims against the tortfeasor's estate and tort claims the decedent could have brought if he had not died. All states have enacted survival statutes, which allow most of the decedent's claims to continue, and wrongful death statutes, which allow for dependents of the decedent to recover from the wrongdoer.

387. Survival statutes vary among the states but they all allow for most legal claims that the decedent could have brought to survive death. The statute is not limited to the tort claim that arose from the injury resulting in death, but most legal actions survive death. To prevent confusion, the statutes name a single legal representative, usually with court approval, that can maintain all legal actions. In addition, the statute of limitation is usually extended for some period of time to allow the legal representative to evaluate potential claims. But, if the decedent dies after a statute of limitation has closed, the survival statute will not reopen that cause of action—only causes of action that were still open before the decedent's death are extended.

388. A wrongful death statute is a third-party action brought by the dependents of the decedent. Each state statute defines the group of eligible dependants, though they usually include spouses, children, adopted children, and parents. As in the survival statute, a legal representative is chosen and the legal representative has a fiduciary duty to represent all of the statutorily defined dependants. Those that are not named in the statute, even though dependent on the decedent during life, are not eligible for recovery.

Chapter 5. Various Damages (Property)

389. A plaintiff may recover all reasonable costs related to the damage or destruction of his property. In the event that the harm is of a continuing nature, such as in a nuisance action, a property owner may request an injunction to prevent the harm from continuing. In the situation where conversion or trespass to chattel can be brought, it is important to note that the damages between these two torts can be different, though, in every other respect, the torts are basically identical. Winning a conversion action results in the plaintiff receiving a judgment for the fair market value of the property that was taken—the only remedy is a forced sale of the property. Prevailing in a trespass to chattels action results in an award for the full fair market value of the damaged property or some lesser amount. The key is recognizing that conversion requires the plaintiff to prove that a forced sale of the property is the only just result and if that is not proven then the case will be lost. For example, a person driving a brand-new car might be upset when someone scratches the car's paint. But if they sue for conversion because they want another new car, they will lose the lawsuit. A trespass to chattels action may recover any reasonable damage to the property, including nominal damages if there was no harm to the property.

Chapter 6. Interference with Collateral Benefits

§1. Insurance

390. The collateral source rule and subrogation are two important issues for plaintiffs that recover the same amount from multiple sources: from the tortfeasor and an insurance policy. The collateral source rule revolves around payments received by plaintiffs for their injuries from collateral sources, which include payments from insurance policies, friends, family, church, or any source other than from the tortfeasor. The collateral source rule prohibits tortfeasors from informing juries of received collateral payments, otherwise, juries might reduce damage awards. Also, tortfeasors are prohibited from reducing amounts they are required to remit to plaintiffs by the amounts of the collateral payments. Though this rule may result in a double recovery to the plaintiff, it is better than the alternative. It is more equitable for injured plaintiffs to benefit over their tortfeasors, who would otherwise pay nothing or something less than the amount of damages they caused. In many states, the traditional collateral source rule has been changed, at least for certain types of plaintiffs. In some of these states, defendants are credited with amounts paid by a collateral source, while in others the jury may be informed of the collateral source.

391. Subrogation is a contractual right that allows insurance companies to recover any damage awards their customers receive in litigation with the tortfeasor. Because those with insurance may receive adequate payment from their insurance company, the insurance company may choose to sue the tortfeasor for recovery of any damages. Also, some plaintiffs that have fully recovered from their insurance company may choose to sue the tortfeasor, hoping for a double recovery. Subrogation prohibits a double recovery by requiring damage awards received in a lawsuit to go to settle the insurance company's claim. Any amount collected above the amount repaid to the insurance company may be kept by the plaintiff after attorney fees have been paid. Workers' Compensation, a state-mandated insurance program, also has statutory subrogation rights that prevent an injured person from a double recovery.

§2. Social Security and Medicare

392. Medicare is the government health care plan provided to social security beneficiaries, and personal injury and worker compensation awards may be subrogated by Medicare under some circumstances.[429] Medicare is a federally funded social program that provides coverage to those over the age of 65 and those under 65 with permanent disabilities. An attorney representing a social security beneficiary in a personal liability lawsuit must immediately contact Medicare and inform them of the potential litigation. By statute, when Medicare provides conditional

429. 42 U.S.C. §1395y(b)(2)(B)(iv).

medical payments it has the right to recover from those that receive payments, "including a beneficiary provider, supplier, physician, attorney, State agency or private insurer that has received a primary payment."[430] In one case, a social security beneficiary was injured by a defective ladder and Medicare paid approximately USD 22,000 in medical claims. The injured person contacted a lawyer, who settled with the ladder manufacturer for USD 25,000. Medicare determined that it was owed approximately USD 10,000 and when the injured person did not make payment, Medicare sued the injured person's attorney and prevailed.[431] Medicare's right to recovery is above all other claims and they are not required to provide notice of their claims.

430. 42 C.F.R. §411.24(g).
431. *U.S. v. Harris*, 2009 WL 891931, slip op. (N.D.W.Va. 2009).

Chapter 7. Other Remedies

§1. Restitution (for Unjust Enrichment)

393. The remedy of restitution is available when the defendant is unjustly enriched by his tortious conduct. Damages are usually measured by the plaintiff's loss while restitution is measured by the defendant's gain. For example, a defendant purchases land from the plaintiff at what the plaintiff believes is a fair price, but the land is worth much more. The defendant then sells the land to a good faith purchaser, making a very large profit. Assuming there was a fraudulent misrepresentation, the appropriate remedy is the defendant's unjust enrichment at the plaintiff's expense. Restitution is often a remedy for fraud, embezzlement, conversion, breach of fiduciary duty, trademark infringement, or copyright infringement. In cases where tortiously obtained property has not been resold, courts will usually impose a constructive trust on the property. This trust, which is a legal fiction, keeps legal title in the name of the tortfeasor but requires him to transfer the property back to the beneficial owner as soon as practicable.

§2. Injunctive Relief

394. Though monetary damages are preferred over equitable remedies, in some cases the appropriate remedy is the injunction. An injunction is an order by a court ordering a person to do something or to stop doing something. Because it is a court order it must be obeyed until it ends or is reversed on appeal. There are no general principles that limit its use and it may be used in many different situations. A common use of the injunction occurs in relation to property rights, as when a person places a structure on the plaintiff's land and the plaintiff asks for an injunction to order the structure off his land. Also, nuisance claims often can result in an injunction when the defendant refuses to stop interfering with the plaintiff's enjoyment of his property

§3. Punitive Damages

395. Punitive damages, also referred to as exemplary damages, are available, but only awarded in exceptional circumstances. One court explained:

> Punitive damages are awarded only in rare instances, to punish and deter outrageous, extreme, egregious behavior. Ordinary negligence, involving inadvertence, mistake or error of judgment will not support an award of punitive damages. Rather, to justify an award of punitive damages, the fact finder must determine that the defendant acted with a culpable state of mind, i.e., with evil motive or reckless indifference to the rights of others. Since a culpable state of

mind is required for an award of punitive damages, evidence of the defendant's knowledge or intention is highly relevant.[432]

Georgia's statute is typical in that "punitive damages may be awarded only in such tort actions in which it is proven by clear and convincing evidence that the defendant's actions showed willful misconduct, malice, fraud, wantonness, oppression, or that entire want of care which would raise the presumption of conscious indifference to consequences."[433] Some states prohibit punitive damages in specific contexts. For example, Alabama prohibits punitive damages in suits against state agencies[434] or against a master when sued under vicarious liability,[435] and several states prohibit them against drug manufacturers.[436] Often attorney fees are available when punitive damages are awarded. Under vicarious liability principles, when an employee engages in conduct that warrants punitive damages, the punitive damages are not imputed to the employer unless the employer also participated in the same conduct that warranted punitive damages against the employee.

396. Because of the concern with excessive punitive damage awards, there have been two major attacks on them. First, many states have enacted statutory caps on punitive damages, often limiting them to a statutory maximum, a ratio between compensatory and punitive damages, or a combination of both. Alabama's code explains that:

> in all civil actions where an entitlement to punitive damages shall have been established under applicable laws, no award of punitive damages shall exceed three times the compensatory damages of the party claiming punitive damages or five hundred thousand dollars ($500,000), whichever is greater.[437]
>
> Some of these statutes place caps only on certain types of plaintiffs, often those injured by medical malpractice. Finally, a few states bifurcate the trial process, creating a separate punitive damage proceeding to determine the amount of punitive damages that will be awarded.[438]

---

432. *Hutchinson v. Penske Truck Leasing Co.*, 876 A.2d 978, 983–984 (Pa. Super. Ct. 2005) (citing *Martin v. Johns-Manville Corp.*, 494 A.2d 1088, 1096–1097 (Pa. 1985), *abrogated on other grounds*, *Kirkbride v. Lisbon Contractors, Inc.*, 555 A.2d 800 (Pa. 1989); *SHV Coal, Inc. v. Continental Grain Co.*, 587 A.2d 702, 704 (Pa. 1991); *Nigro v. Remington Arms Co., Inc.*, 637 A.2d 983, 989 (Pa. Super. Ct. 1993), *abrogated on other grounds*, *Aldridge v. Edmunds*, 750 A.2d 292, 297 (Pa. 2000)).
433. Ga. Code Ann., §51-12-5.1(b).
434. Ala. Code §6-11-26.
435. Ala. Code §6-11-27.
436. Kan. Stat. Ann. 60-3701; Ohio Rev. Code Ann. §2307.80(C); Or. Rev. Stat. §§31.740.
437. Ala. Code 1975 §6-11-21(a).
438. *See* AS §09.17.020(c). At the separate proceeding to determine the amount of punitive damages to be awarded, the fact finder may consider:

    1. the likelihood at the time of the conduct that serious harm would arise from the defendant's conduct;
    2. the degree of the defendant's awareness of the likelihood described in (1) of this subsection;
    3. the amount of financial gain the defendant gained or expected to gain as a result of the defendant's conduct;

397. The second limitation is based on a series of decisions by the Supreme Court of the United States, limiting punitive damages based on federal constitutional due process grounds. In one case the plaintiff was awarded USD 1 million in compensatory damages for their emotional harm and USD 145 million in punitive damages. The Supreme Court held that the punitive damage award violated the federal constitution and suggested that a smaller ratio between the compensatory and punitive award would be appropriate. The Court explained that in cases with smaller amounts of compensatory damages, a larger compensatory/punitive damage ratio might be more appropriate.[439]

4. the duration of the conduct and any intentional concealment of the conduct;
5. the attitude and conduct of the defendant upon discovery of the conduct;
6. the financial condition of the defendant; and
7. the total deterrence of other damages and punishment imposed on the defendant as a result of the conduct, including compensatory and punitive damages awards to persons in situations similar to those of the plaintiff and the severity of the criminal penalties to which the defendant has been or may be subjected.

439. *State Farm Mut Auto. Ins. Co. v. Campbell*, 538 U.S. 408 (2003).

Selected Bibliography

Tort Law in General

Dobbs, Dan. *The Law of Torts*. St. Paul, MN: West Group, 2000.
Harper, Fowler, Fleming James & Oscar Gray. *Harper, James and Gray on Torts*. New York: Aspen Publishers, 2009.
Holmes, Jr., Oliver. *The Common Law*. Boston: Little, Brown & Co., 1881.
Restatement of the Law Second, Torts. Philadelphia: American Law Institute, 1965.
Speiser, Stuart, Charles Krause & Alfred Gans. *The American Law of Torts*. St. Paul, MN: Thompson-West, 2003.

Liability for One's Own Acts

Prosser, William. "Privacy." *California Law Review* 48 (1960): 383.
Restatement Third, Torts: Liability for Physical and Emotional Harm. Philadelphia: American Law Institute, 2005.

Liability for Acts of Others

"Independent Contractors." *American Jurisprudence*. Vol. 41, §8. St. Paul, MN: Thompson-West, 2008.
Baty, Thomas. "The Basis of Responsibility." *Juridical Review* 32 (1920): 159.
Restatement of the Law Third, Agency. Philadelphia: American Law Institute, 2006.

Forms of Strict Liability

Eades, Ronald W. *Mastering Products Liability*. Durham, NC: Carolina Academic Press, 2008.
Owen, David G. *Products Liability Law*. St. Paul, MN: Thompson-West, 2008.
Restatement of the Law Third, Torts: Products Liability. Philadelphia: American Law Institute, 1998.
Uniform Commercial Code, Article 2. Chicago: National Conference of Commissioners on Uniform State Laws, 2003.

Defenses and Exception Clauses

Gardner, Steven. "Contributory Negligence, Comparative Negligence, and Stare Decisis in North Carolina." *Campbell Law Review* 18 (1996): 1.

Selected Bibliography

Causation

Hart, H.L.A. & Anthony Honoré. *Causation in the Law*. Oxford: Clarendon Press, 1962.

Restatement of the Law Third, Torts: Apportionment of Liability. Philadelphia: American Law Institute, 2000.

Remedies

Dobbs, Dan. *Dobbs Law of Remedies: Damages, Equity, Restitution*. 2nd ed. St. Paul, MN: West Publishing, 1993.

Restatement of the Law Third, Torts: Apportionment of Liability. Philadelphia: American Law Institute, 2000.

Index

The numbers here refer to paragraph numbers.

Index

Index

www.ingramcontent.com/pod-product-compliance
Lightning Source LLC
LaVergne TN
LVHW011133300926
849160LV00008B/628
9789403562407